# A.W.

Compiled and Ed...

# A

# DISRUPTIVE

# FAITH

EXPECT

GOD

TO

INTERRUPT

YOUR

LIFE

**Regal**

From Gospel Light
Ventura, California, U.S.A.

Published by Regal

From Gospel Light

Ventura, California, U.S.A.

*www.regalbooks.com*

Printed in the U.S.A.

Library of Congress Cataloging-in-Publication Data

Tozer, A. W. (Aiden Wilson), 1897-1963.

A disruptive faith : expect God to interrupt your life / A.W. Tozer.

p. cm.

Includes bibliographical references and index.

ISBN 978-0-8307-5761-9 (trade paper : alk. paper)

1. Faith. 2. Trust in God—Christianity. 3. Christian life. I. Title.

BT771.3.T69 2011

248.4—dc22

2011001839

Rights for publishing this book outside the U.S.A. or in non-English languages are
administered by Gospel Light Worldwide, an international not-for-profit ministry.
For additional information, please visit www.glww.org, email info@glww.org, or write
to Gospel Light Worldwide, 1957 Eastman Avenue, Ventura, CA 93003, U.S.A.

To order copies of this book and other Regal products in bulk quantities,
please contact us at 1-800-446-7735.

# CONTENTS

# INTRODUCTION

*Worship is no longer worship when it reflects the culture around us more than the Christ within us.*

A. W. TOZER

Throughout his ministry, Dr. A. W. Tozer constantly drew fresh water from old wells. He followed the track of those who hungered and thirsted after God, often picking up clues from their lives that increased his desire to understand what it means to grow and mature in Christ. Even more significant, he was devoted to meditating on the Word of God until he could hear it speak God's truths to his heart. As a result, he has much to teach those of like spirit and much to teach on the subject of true biblical faith as found in the book of Hebrews.

Tozer was quite fond of the saying, from the old Lutherans, "Faith is a perturbing thing." You will find this concept woven all through this book. In one chapter, Tozer points out that faith is a journey for the heart. Contrary to what some teach today, faith is not the destination. In addition, faith does not create things. Although entire faith ministries are devoted to teaching people how they can get what they want from God, according to Dr. Tozer, faith does not create anything. Rather, faith is the spiritual organ by which we can see what God has created. The purpose of faith is for us to penetrate the visible and see into the invisible reality, which is God. When the Scriptures say, "We walk by faith, not by sight," it is referring to this invisible, mystical aspect of God's creation.

The theme of this book is the disruptive aspect of faith, as broken down into three basic areas. First, for the unsaved person, there is the initial disturbance of faith. The faith of the Bible contradicts the way of life outside of Jesus Christ. In every aspect, faith disrupts the life of sin and rebellion against God. It contradicts everything about the natural man. The beginning of faith is a disturbance—a deep sense of conviction over sin.

Second, for the growing Christian, there is the ongoing disruption of his or her complacency. Our tendency is to get so caught up with what we do that we fail to see what God has done. Faith leads us and allows us to gaze into the face of God and rest. Biblical faith prods us forward and challenges us to rest completely in the finished work of Jesus Christ.

Third, for the mature Christian, there is the steady walk of faith that usually leads down a disturbing and disruptive path toward deeper experience of God. An example from Scripture would be the case of the three Hebrew children—Shadrach, Meshach and Abednego—who were put into a fiery furnace. Their faith got them into trouble. What they said to Nebuchadnezzar is characteristic of those who walk by faith and not by sight. "If it be so, our God whom we serve is able to deliver us from the burning fiery furnace, and he will deliver us out of thine hand, O king. But if not, be it known unto thee, O king, that we will not serve thy gods, nor worship the golden image which thou hast set up" (Dan. 3:17-18). Although their faith brought them to the furnace, it also saw them through that terrible ordeal. In the midst of that fire, they experienced, by faith, the actual presence of God.

Throughout history, men and women of faith have gotten into trouble. If you are walking by faith, you are going to go contrary to the ways of the world. Faith will challenge your circumstances and prod you in the direction of persistently following the leadership of the Holy Spirit.

Obviously, Dr. Tozer had a different view of this whole concept of faith than those who say that by faith we can create the life we want. Genuine faith, Tozer believed, leads to a disquietude that begins to wean us from this life and prepares us for the life to come. The work and ministry of the Holy Spirit within the life of the believer has this goal in mind all the time: to bring sons and daughters unto glory.

This book, *A Disruptive Faith*, is a treasure both for the young Christian just starting out in the race of faith and for the veteran believer who is getting closer to the finish line. Like any good coach, Dr. Tozer continually redirects to the right course; provides the way to get around the inevitable obstacles, which is the reality of our threefold enemy—the world, the flesh and the devil; and delivers the hard truths of what it takes to go the distance in a contrary world and finish well. His unfolding of the faith-life, from the book of Hebrews, will cheer you on to cross the finish line in victory.

James L. Snyder

# 1

# THE GENESIS OF OUR CHRISTIAN FAITH

*But one in a certain place testified, saying, What is man, that thou art mindful of him? or the son of man, that thou visitest him?*

HEBREWS 2:6

Where does our Christian faith come from? Depending on the answer, a person will go in the right direction or the wrong direction. Unfortunately, many teachers, if not giving wrong answers, are at least giving incomplete answers to this vital question and are, ultimately, leading people astray.

I want to state right up front that authentic faith begins with an understanding of our place in God's thinking. The writer to the Hebrews asked, "What is man, that thou art mindful of him? Or the Son of Man, that Thou visitest him?" (Heb. 2:6), quoting from Psalm 8:4. This is actually one question, but I want to set before you some ground rules about this question.

First, this is not an academic question asked merely for the sake of argument. Scripture does not lend itself to anything merely academic. This is an explanation. The man of God gazes at the sky, is overwhelmed by what he sees and puts this question to God: "What is man?" To know that God thinks about us is the beginning of our journey of faith.

Second, in searching the Scriptures, you will never find anything there for the sake of satisfying the curious. God never propounds mere speculation. You will find that everything in the Bible is practical, moral and spiritual. Each book of the Bible has a specific purpose to it. The specific purpose of the book of Hebrews, for example, is to take men and women who were alienated from God and reconcile them to Him. Very simply put, the message of Hebrews is to make sinful men good, to take men neglecting their future lives and persuade them to become concerned about their future.

## Fixed in God's Mind

The word "mindful," in the question, "What is man, that thou art mindful of him?" implies that man is a fixture in God's mind and comes to His remembrance continually. God's weakness for mankind is the only eccentricity of our great God, and I say that with a great deal of reverence. I can understand why God did most everything that I know He did. It is easy to see why He might do some things, but it is extremely difficult to understand why God should love mankind and why man should be such a fixture in God's mind. It is one of the strangest phenomena in the universe.

Associated with this is God's inability to shake off His burden for the human race. Although self-imposed, this burden is no less a burden. Mankind fixed in God's mind is as a nail driven into hard wood, and God cannot escape it. I do not know that God wants to escape it, but I know that the nature of God is such that He cannot escape it. God's love for mankind is a hurt—a wound of the heart. Man's treachery has deeply wounded Him, but He is caught in the sweet and painful meshes of His own love. He is impaled, so to speak, on the point of His own great love for mankind.

I believe this is true. I believe it in my living, in my preaching, in my prayers. I believe that it can be said of man, "God is mindful of him." Just as a mother is mindful of a child, God is mindful of man, only infinitely more, for it's possible for a mother to forsake and forget her child. Usually, a mother's love will last; but sometimes even a mother's love gives way. But the love of God is such that it can never end. God remains caught in the web of His own mighty love. Man, with all of his treachery, all of his sinfulness, imprudence and evil, remains a fixture in the mind of God.

Man is God's image, pride, responsibility and problem. He is all this. God does not sleep, but I am sure that if He slept, He could not sleep because He is haunted by the treachery of man and caught in the web of His love for man and His pride in man. He feels himself responsible for man, though certainly there can be no moral responsibility. Man forfeited all that when he sinned. Yet God takes on Himself the responsibility. Groaning under this pressure, God says, "Behold, I am pressed under you, as a cart is pressed that is full of sheaves" (Amos 2:13).

## Despite Man's Frailty

It was man's frailty that made the psalmist ask, "When I consider thy heavens . . . what is man?" (Ps. 8:3-4). This question, of course, must be answered from God's viewpoint.

The biblical perspective is that man is likened to grass, to flowers, to a breath that you take in and then expel and it is gone. He is likened to a vapor that lies over the hill in the morning but is gone as soon as the sun is up. He is likened to a flower that blooms so beautifully and brings so many exclamations of delight from those who see it. Yet, in a few days, it is a faded, limp thing nobody cares to see anymore. Man is like the grass that grows up in the morning and withers before nightfall.

David, the man of God that he was, declared, "But truly *as* the LORD liveth, and *as* thy soul liveth, there is but a step between me and death" (1 Sam. 20:3). Man, in all of his fullness, is only a step away from death. Yet, this frail creature plagues the mind of God continually.

Why should the eternal God be caught in the love of that which is so frail? I do not know. I only know that it is true.

The only thing that equals man's frailty is man's ignorance. The evidence of this is all around. We see it in idolatry. We see it with the philosophers.

The five unanswered questions are, *Where did we come from? How did we get here? What are we? Why are we here?* and *Where are we going?* These questions cannot be answered except by going to the Bible for the answers. Man, in his ignorance, does not know and can never discover the answers by himself.

Into this Universe and why not knowing,
Nor whence, like Water willy-nilly flowing:
And out of it, as Wind along the Waste,
I know not whither, willy-nilly blowing.[1]

We do not know where we came from nor how we got here. Of course we know the facts of our birth, but we do not know the mystery that makes it possible for human life to be born. We do not know what we are apart from God. We do not know why we are here apart from our instruction from the New Testament; and we do not know whither we are going.

From a human standpoint, this frailty of man argues against love. However, man's frailty cannot displace him from God's thinking about him continually. Human reason dictates that this frailty of mankind should make him beyond the realm of love, and yet, God's love overrides any hint of unworthiness on man's part.

## Despite Man's Iniquity

Man's frailty is not the worst that can be said about him. I could see why God might love that which is frail. I could see how God might love that which is ignorant; but I cannot see how God can love that which is iniquitous. And yet, man's iniquity and God's love are found in the same paragraph and sometimes in the same verse.

History is man's indictment. Just read history and you will find the evidence that man is exceedingly wicked. Our daily conduct is the evidence of our guilt. Any theologian who does not believe in the fall of man and the iniquity of the human race has only to pick up tomorrow's morning newspaper or listen to the latest news report. Man's daily conduct is all the evidence the world needs. God needs to convict man because man is guilty and has betrayed himself in the very thing that marks him as godlike. He has betrayed himself in thought, truth and virtue. He has betrayed himself spiritually, intellectually and morally. He has proved himself unworthy to live.

Some cannot understand why God lets man die; but I cannot understand why God lets man live, because he has forfeited all right to live, by his iniquity. Yet, in spite of all of this, man is a fixture in God's mind. God cannot escape the great love of His heart for the human race.

I once talked to a young man who said he could not believe or understand how God could love him. Then he read in Genesis 6:6 that God saw the wickedness of man and it grieved Him in His heart. He said, "I saw that only love could grieve, and you do not grieve unless you love." We can suffer many other ways. A man can break a leg and suffer. A man can lose property and suffer. But nobody can ever grieve except he has love. When my friend read that man had grieved God in His heart, he knew then that God loved him. That is good reasoning, and a good way to look at things. God loves us or He never would grieve over us.

In the Scriptures, Jesus was called "a man of sorrows" (Isa. 53:3). What was the sorrow Jesus bore? What was the pain in His mind, in His heart? It was our pain—the pain of our sins. This pain knows no ease and makes God restless and eager. All of God's acts of mercy come out of this pain in His heart. His mercy is not drawn out; it is forced out by love. Saying, "I do not think God loves me—I am not worthy of it," would be like a field saying, "Do not rain on me. I am not worthy of it."

The clouds, when pregnant with rain, do not ask whether the field is worthy; but when certain conditions develop, it rains regardless, and it rains on the just and on the unjust alike (see Matt. 5:45). It rains on the city streets and the meadows in the country. That is how the love of God is. He loves you not because you are worthy, but because He is God and you are a fixture in His mind. You are spiritually depraved, intellectually blind and morally corrupt. But God says, "Yet will I not forget thee" (Isa. 49:15). I believe that, and I base my life on that truth.

We used to sing an old camp meeting song called "Sweet Is the Promise, I Will Not Forget Thee," by Charles H. Gabriel (1856-1932):

Sweet is the promise "I will not forget thee,"
Nothing can molest or turn my soul away;
E'en though the night be dark within the valley,
Just beyond is shining an eternal day.

Trusting the promise "I will not forget thee,"
Onward I will go with songs of joy and love,
Though earth despise me,
Though my friends forsake me,
I shall be remembered in my home above.

When at the golden portals I am standing,
All my tribulations, all my sorrows past;
How sweet to hear the blessed proclamation,
"Enter, faithful servant, welcome home at last."

I will not forget thee or leave thee,
In My hands I'll hold thee,
In My arms I'll fold thee,
I will not forget thee or leave thee;
I am thy Redeemer, I will care for thee.

When a man has a sharp pain that will not let up, either in his body or in his heart, he does not forget it. When someone dies, we grieve, and it becomes a fixture in our hearts and we do not forget the person. The pain in God's heart is all the reminder He would need that we are ignorant and iniquitous and frail and alienated and helpless. God's passion for man, pure as it is, drives forward to man's redemption. God has stretched out His hand toward us. Because we are a fixture in His mind, He visited us. "What is man, that thou art mindful of him? or the son of man that thou visitest him?" (Heb. 2:6).

## What Drives God's Purpose

We talk about history and God working in human history. But what lies behind the development of God's purpose is found in the unfathomable mystery of His love for us.

Let me give you a couple of examples about what lies behind the development of purpose. Say that a young couple is preparing to get married. They have known each other for six months or maybe a year. The relationship has slowly developed and now they are going to get married. The day of the wedding has come, presents are arranged, the flowers are bought. Everything has been prepared, and the bride is ready to put on her wedding dress. She sits calmly back, stony-faced, and says, "I am getting married this evening. It is the development in the history of my husband's plan." You would think she was a dead fish as she sits back and talks about the historical development of the masculine plan.

Some might say, "What is the matter with you, honey? Don't you love him?" You do not talk about marriage in that way. You talk about it in the language of emotion, of feeling, of love.

Once, when I was visiting New York City, I happened to see a couple carrying a little baby in a basket. I would guess he was nine months old; and as they came out of Toffenetti's restaurant, everybody who passed by looked at the little baby and smiled. Even stiff New Yorkers looked down and smiled. It did not take me long to find him, and I was looking down and making eyes at him, and he was laughing back. Where did that baby come from?

Biologists, physiologists and all the rest would make charts to explain that baby. That is the best they can do. But the mystery behind his birth will never be known, even though his physical part can be explained. That is an awful way to think of a baby—as a biped anthropoid. Normally, we think of a baby in terms of affection and warmth and love. A baby that was raised in a laboratory where there were only scientists with mirrors on the top of their heads, why, he would be a zombie, not a human being. Babies have to have love.

Scientists have weighed in on this and informed us that you should never love a baby. If he cries, let him cry. Teach him self-assurance. My wife and I paid no attention to that kind of advice. We loved our babies anyhow and let them cling. Shortly after that, the experts reversed their opinion, and now they are teaching just the opposite. They say, above all things, love your baby.

Do you really have to tell a mother to love her baby? Do you have to send her to school and take two semesters to learn to love her baby? All she has to do is see the little thing lying there all wrinkled up and red, working on his thumb. Two hours old and she is wild about him and thinks he looks like her husband immediately. She loves him without any experts explaining to her how to do it.

My old Dutch grandmother always said, "Every crow thinks her young are the blackest." You do not need an education to love your baby. You love him because he is your baby and not necessarily because he is lovable.

## Fulfilled Love

What brought Jesus Christ to die? The Scriptures record, "Thou visitest him" (Heb. 2:6). Why did He visit us? Was it that He might carry out the eternal purpose? Yes, but that is not the way to look at it. He visited us because we were a fixture in His mind. He came for us as a mother wakes in the morning and runs into the room to see if her baby is all right. It was love that brought Him down to die. God's anxious, restless love was incarnated in human flesh. This accounts for the character of Christ and for His attitude toward people and His tireless labor for them. This ultimately accounts for His dying for them. He never would have died merely to fulfill a purpose in history. Had God laid a chart out on the wall and said, "Not this way or that way, but this way . . ." I doubt if Christ would have died to fulfill the purposes on some chart. But He did die to fulfill the affections of the heart. That was another matter. That is why He died and that is what gave us Calvary.

Our Lord's great pain for us compelled Him to come down to earth. Calvary was a pain. The nails were painful. And the hanging there, perspiring in the hot sun, with the flies, must have been a painful, awful experience. But one pain was bigger than the other. It drove Him to endure the little pain. The greater pain was His pain of loving. He loved us and died for us. He endured the pain of death because the greater pain of love betrayed His love for us; and we turned and looked at Him and walked away and cared not for Him. To love and not be loved in return is one of the most exquisite pains in the entire repertoire of painfulness. So He came, He lived, He loved and He died; and death could not destroy that love. It is still a fixture in His mind. But someday that love is going to be fully satisfied.

Did you ever consider this marvelous passage of Scripture? "He shall see the travail of his soul, and shall be satisfied: by his knowledge shall my righteous servant justify many; for he shall bear their iniquities" (Isa. 53:11). What did the writer mean by that? He meant the same thing that Jesus meant when He said, "A woman when she is in travail hath sorrow, because her hour is come: but as soon as she is delivered of the child, she remembereth no more the anguish, for joy that a man is born into the world" (John 16:21). So says the Scripture of Jesus, "He shall see of the travail of his soul, and shall be satisfied" (Isa. 53:11).

## Where Our Faith Begins

Man, as long as he is sinning, is a pain in God's heart. When he turns from his sin to God, he is a satisfaction in God's heart. Everybody is one of these two things—either a pain in God's heart or a satisfaction in God's heart. Christ is either pained by your rejection or pleased by your acceptance. He is happy and satisfied that He has found you, or He is grief-stricken still that you have not yet found Him.

Remember, men are fixtures in God's mind. They are there forever. God cannot shake loose this eternal fixture. The human race is there. We are there even if there be pain in His heart or joy in His heart. I, for my part, want to bring joy to the Lord Jesus Christ.

The foundation of my faith in God is knowing that I am a fixture in His mind. This is where my faith begins and it is where I begin to understand my place in God's thinking. When I understand how God thinks about me, it starts me on the journey of faith. I can trust the one who has my best interests in mind for the longest period of time.

### Trusting Jesus
Edgar P. Stites (1836–1921)

Simply trusting ev'ry day
Trusting through a stormy way;
Even when my faith is small,
Trusting Jesus, that is all.

Trusting as the moments fly,
Trusting as the days go by;
Trusting him whate'er befall,
Trusting Jesus, that is all.

Brightly doth his Spirit shine
Into this poor heart of mine;
While he leads I cannot fall;
Trusting Jesus, that is all.

Singing if my way is clear;
Praying if the path be drear;
If in danger, for him call;
Trusting Jesus, that is all.

Trusting him while life shall last,
Trusting him till earth be past;
Till within the jasper wall;
Trusting Jesus, that is all.

**Note**

1. Edward FitzGerald (1809–1883), from *The Rubáaiyat of Omar Khayyam.*

2

# THE CONFIRMATION OF OUR FAITH

*God, who at sundry times and in divers manners spake*
*in time past unto the fathers by the prophets,*
*hath in these last days spoken unto us by his Son.*

HEBREWS 1:1-2

The book of Hebrews teaches that God speaks through His Word by the eternal Son. Understanding the purpose of Scripture will go a long way toward integrating it into our daily life. Quite plainly, the purpose of the Scripture is to authenticate and confirm in the Christian that faith which was once delivered unto the saints. From this we understand that the place of God's Word in the Christian's life determines the quality and authenticity of his faith.

Christian faith is not so much what you say you believe, but how you behave in a consistent manner. My Christian faith will always reveal itself in my Christian behavior when I am least conscious of it. These days there is so much ado about faith without any scriptural context. For all practical purposes, the "man of faith" is being exalted as a Christian celebrity. This is an oxymoron, defying not only the plain teaching of the Bible, but also Church history and Christian biography.

23

## Authentic, Unwavering Faith

The supreme purpose of the book of Hebrews, the reason the Holy Spirit inspired it to be written, was to confirm the wavering Hebrew Christians in their faith.

I will not surrender to the idea that the book of Hebrews was written for unconverted people. This is a heresy sprung up as a necessary dodge to take care of another heresy. When one heresy comes, another one has to come to hide it, and then another one bigger than those two has to come to hide them. Soon you have a whole chain of heresies. To make allowance for certain wrong beliefs, certain brethren explain that the book of Hebrews is not for Christians at all. It is simply for people who were hanging around the outside and not yet saved. But the book of Hebrews was written to confirm Hebrew Christians in their faith. And the way they were confirmed was that Christ, the eternal Son, is presented as being all in all. The writer goes to great lengths to show this all-sufficiency of Christ.

## A New and Living Way

It is a strengthening thing to know that although Christianity grew out of Judaism, it is not dependent upon Judaism at all. Jesus, our Lord, said, "And no man putteth new wine into old bottles; else the new wine will burst the bottles, and be spilled, and the bottles shall perish" (Luke 5:37). What He meant was that you do not put Christianity into Judaism.

A great gulf existed between Judaism and Christianity—between the Judaism of the Old Testament, the Mosaic order, and Christianity. A man is born of his mother but grows up to full manhood, and when his mother dies, he continues on independent of her though he was born of her. Just so the Christian faith was born of Judaism, but it is independent of Judaism even as it rests upon the same Lord that Judaism rested upon. Judaism foreshadowed Christianity, but Christianity was not and is not dependent upon it.

The book of Hebrews stands in its own grand strength—a temple where stands the eternal Son, the High Priest of God, forever. This letter begins with the word "God." It begins where everything begins; it begins with God. Genesis is the great book of creation, and it begins by saying, "In the beginning God," or "God in the beginning." This book of Hebrews is the great book of redemption and begins with the word "God."

All things begin and end in God—time and space, matter and motion, life and law, form and order, all purposes and all plans, all succession and all procession. Everything moves out from God and finally returns back to Him. We must open our eyes to see that whatever does not begin in God and end in God is not worthy of our attention, for we have been made in the image of God. Personally, I believe it is more comprehensive than that. It may even be a snare for us. Any interest that does not have God in it is our enemy at last. We were created for God, made in His image, and our chief end is to serve Him, admire Him, worship Him and enjoy Him forever.

Therefore, anything you do or plan to do or have any interest in, which does not begin in God, is a snare to you and is a result of the fall of man, your fall in Adam. Any plan, any project, any activity, any philosophy you may hold, any beliefs you may have, any motivations in life that do not begin in God and end in God, are your enemy. Beware that you do not cast in your lot with mortality. We, the children of the light and of eternity, are called of God to live immortal lives. That is, we are called to live in the light of immortality. You must be very careful you do not hear the siren voice of the world sounding and calling you from the contemplations of things immortal to give your time and cast in your lot with mortality.

## No Contradiction

Notice these words: "God . . . spake in time past" (Heb. 1:1). God had been speaking to the human race over a period of 4,000 years when these words were written. The race had separated itself from God, fled from the Garden and held itself incommunicado. The human race had its gods and its altars, and mumbled its prayers. It was alienated from God and did not have God in its mind. God was only a tradition. The voice that sounded in the Garden was silent—not that it was actually silent, but they did not hear it. So the ages might have continued until both man and nature failed and were no more. But God came and spoke, breaking the silence. He spoke to Adam in the Garden; He spoke after the Garden; He spoke to Noah, Abraham and to David, all down the years. Therefore, all the prophets since the world began heard the voice of God. God was speaking, as the Scriptures here say, "at sundry times."

God spoke to various persons at various times, but always His words accorded with all His other words. If you give too much attention to a word and force yourself to examine and analyze it, soon you will have a dead bug in your hand and you will not be able to believe what it does mean. It is the same with Scripture. If we press in too hard and bore into it too far and examine it too much, especially if we do not walk in the light of it, then it becomes darkness to us.

Then the Bible must be divided rightly, which Peter commends of Paul as the wisdom given him by God. Of Paul, he said, "As also in all his epistles, speaking in them of these things; in which are some things hard to be understood, which they that are unlearned and unstable wrest, as they do also the other scriptures, unto their own destruction" (2 Pet. 3:16). Because Paul said, "Study to shew thyself approved unto God, a workman that needeth not to be ashamed, rightly dividing the word of truth" (2 Tim. 2:15), Bible teachers have gotten out their scalpels, butcher knives and meat cleavers and have been at it now for a generation, cleaving the holy Word of God into bits, slicing it into parts and laying it out, quivering and bleeding on the blocks.

Keep in mind that all of the Bible is for you and me. It may not all be about you and me, but it is all for you and me. This is one of the standing rules of the Moody Bible Institute, which is a good rule to keep in mind. When God spoke to various persons at various times, His words were always accorded with His other words.

Some have tried to bring differences of opinion between Paul and James. They say that James believed in works, and Paul believed in faith. But what they do not know is that Paul believed in faith and works, and James believed in works and faith. Both believed in faith and works, only they stated it a little differently. One man saw they were trying to believe without obeying, and the other man saw they were trying to obey without believing, and both rebuked the embryonic Christians for their failure.

God always says the same things to people, wherever He says it. God, being one and always speaking out of His own unitarian nature, always says the same thing to everybody; He speaks the same grace and the same love and the same justice and the same holiness and the same righteousness and the same goodness. Father, Son and Holy Ghost always speak out of their one nature; they say the same thing wherever they are saying it.

I have noticed a widening and increasing revelation over the passage of years. The Lord spoke cryptically to the serpent. He told of warfare between the serpent and the seed of the woman. He told of a bruised head and a bruised heel of the victorious Champion who was to come. He told Eve of sorrow in child-bearing and of her social status, her place in the family. To Adam, He told of cursed ground and the necessity of toil and, finally, the coming of death. To Cain and Abel, He told of forgiveness through sacrifice. To Noah, He told of grace and the order of nature in government. To Abraham, He told of the coming of the seed, the Redeemer who was to come to make atonement for the race. To Moses, He gave the Law and the Levitical order and told of the coming Prophet who was like unto Moses, but so unlike him, and so superior to him.

## Same Voice, Different Method

So God spoke "at sundry times" and "in divers manners." He always said about the same thing, but He did not always say it in the same manner. Somebody might shout across the back fence to you or call you on the telephone or send you a telegram, write you a letter, whisper to you or yell at you. It is the same person trying to get through to you, but in different ways, depending upon the circumstances. So God spoke, and He spoke in "divers manners." That word "divers" is the old word for "different." He spoke in different manners to different persons at different times.

## Adam and Eve

God spoke to Adam and Eve by a soft, gentle voice as He walked in the Garden in the cool of the day. I do not know how you feel, or if you have ever thought of it, but I will never be a totally happy man until I hear that voice sounding again and know that I will never be away from its presence. That gentle voice of God sounding out in the garden in the cool of the day will someday sound throughout the entire universe and bring into one all His ransomed children.

## Abraham

God also spoke to Abraham once in a deep sleep. Do not ask me how He spoke, I do not know. The matter of the technique of inspiration has always escaped me. I wish I could do what some of my learned brethren do—decide how they want to believe about a thing and then quietly rule out all the other evidence. It would be such a comfortable thing to know everything, never to be bothered and never to sit in the middle and say, "Do not ask me. Lord, thou knowest. I do not." When it comes to how God spoke to a man in a deep sleep, I do not know. Furthermore, no one living knows. Just some people who think they know. Regardless, Abraham heard the voice of God and recorded what he heard.

## Moses and the Prophets

Then there was Moses. God spoke to Moses out of the burning bush; He spoke on the mountain; He spoke by writing with His finger on the stone tablet. And there were prophets who heard God speaking in dreams and visions, and God talked to them by signs and symbols. But always, God, whom the world thinks is silent, was not silent at all. It is a great error to believe in the silence of God. God is only silent where men cannot hear. The voice of God is sounding throughout His world continually, and the man who hears it may be a prophet, an apostle, a missionary, a reformer, a soul-winner or a Bible teacher.

# The Inspiration of Scripture

No one can believe with more certainty in the inspiration of the Scriptures than I do. The Scriptures, which speak loudly to those who have ears to hear, can lie silent for a thousand years, read by minds that cannot hear and will never know what they mean. The Ethiopian eunuch was traveling along, reading from the book of Isaiah—one of the most self-explanatory chapters in the whole of Scripture (see Isa. 53:7-8)—and yet he had no idea what it meant. It took the Holy Spirit, speaking through Philip, to come and reveal it to him (see Acts 8:26-35).

## Understanding Comes Through the Holy Spirit

I believe it is possible to read my Bible, and read it regularly, and yet not know what it means until I hear a voice in it. When I hear a voice in it, that voice never says anything contrary to itself. But it speaks through it. The voice is a trumpet through which God Almighty speaks. You can translate and retranslate a thousand ways, but if you are not able to hear His voice sounding the trumpet, you might just as well not have the trumpet.

We have so many translations of the Scriptures these days, and it is all right. Let them come. I am the world's greatest target for a new translation. Just as soon as one is out, I must have it. I have whole shelves of them. I do not get any help out of them particularly, because I realize God can tell me to do something in 40 different ways.

The Lord says, "Go and apologize to brother Jones." There's only one thing for me to do to get out of my difficulty and that is to go and apologize to brother Jones, to humble myself and apologize. I can say it in the modern, snappy slang of the *Philips* translation. I can say it in the noble language of the *King James Version*. I can say it in this garbled *New English Version*. I can say it any way I want to say it, but it does not make any difference. If I do not go and apologize, I have failed God and myself. So it does not make any difference to me what translation you use. Incidentally, I do not believe the devil ever translated the Bible. I do not think I have accepted any devil-translated Bibles at all, in spite of my eager-beaver brethren who try to make me think the devil has translated the Scriptures.

Here is what I am trying to get at: God spoke in "divers manners"—He spoke to various people in various ways. And then God caused some things to be written down in the Book. And that Book is the final test of all doctrine, of all morality, of all Christian ethics, of all beliefs for this world and the world to come. That Book can lie dead as a rock until a voice is heard speaking through it, until the Holy Spirit causes it to come alive to our hearts. Scripture must be understood through the Holy

Spirit who inspired it. In some translations it says "in many fragments." I think they are right in that the whole thing is imperfect and incomplete, and they all lead up to something and wait for something. I am thinking of the Old Testament now. The Old Testament is like a house without a door. It calls for something else. "In these last days," says the Holy Spirit, God has "spoken unto us by his Son" (Heb. 1:2).

## Jesus Is the Eternal Word

God, who in olden times spoke to the prophets, is now speaking to us through His Son. Before, He spoke through many voices; but now He is speaking through one voice, the voice of His Son, Jesus Christ our Lord. To miss this voice, Jesus Christ, is to miss hearing the voice of God. In anticipation of this, during His ministry, Jesus said, "I am the way, the truth, and the life: no man cometh unto the Father, but by me" (John 14:6). The Way has now become the Voice.

I like to think that the Word of God is Son-wise, if we could use such a word. God spoke Sonly. He spoke in His Son to His people, and the Son is called the Word. God spoke and Mary conceived, and the Word became the baby and then a man. This was God speaking. This was the eternal Son, the eternal generation of the Son, which was before the world was. God's eternal Son, equal with the Father, was less than the Father in His manhood, but equal to the Father in His Godhead—co-eternal, co-equal, of one substance with the Father. Now He became flesh, and when He became flesh, He did not cease to be what He had been: the Word, the medium through which God spoke to His universe. Through whom He is now speaking.

In reading the Gospels and the New Testament, you will know that the Spirit of Jesus Christ is in it and has inspired it. You are not hearing only words; you are hearing the eternal Word. You are seeing not only light, you are seeing the light that lighteth every man that cometh into the world (see John 1:4). You are hearing a voice from another world. Not an echo, but a voice from another world. Previously, He spoke in many voices, but now He speaks in the one. The message of the book of Hebrews is that Jesus Christ is God speaking. He no longer speaks in a scattered, tentative, imperfect way, but in a clear and audible and full and final way. What He is saying to all who believe today, wherever there is faith, is the High Priest, the eternal Son.

It is where high the heavenly Temple stands,
The house of God not made with hands,
A great high priest our nature wears,
The Guardian of mankind appears.[1]

## God Speaking to You

Instead of hiding as Adam hid behind the trees in the Garden, some are hiding behind the tree of theology; others are hiding behind the tree of philosophy; still others are hiding behind the tree of reason. Everyone must come out from behind those trees and let God speak. God has spoken to us in His Son, and what He is saying is not a philosophical thing, not a thing of the reasoning mind, but a thing of the heart. The question of the eternal Son and His relation to us, and our relation to Him is a moral question, something of conscience and conduct and obedience and loyalty. Jesus Christ, who appears so big in the book of Hebrews, is greater than angels, greater than Moses, greater than Melchizedek, greater than all the high priests. And all our future is bound up with Him, and He is bound up in the future of each one of us. We cannot escape Him; we cannot appeal to God apart from Him.

In the meantime, we stand in a vacuum. There is no such vacuum between a speaking God who spoke and a speaking God who will speak, but who is now silent. There never has been such a bracket in any time in history, and there is none now. The God who spoke is speaking, and the words He speaks will judge you in the last day.

The God who spoke is speaking still, and He will continue speaking. He is saying to us that we are to examine ourselves. We are to put our confidence in the blood that was shed and the body that was broken. And we are to believe in the great High Priest who is gone up on high—with our names on His breast and His hands and His shoulders—to be our High Priest forever at the right hand of God, until He fulfills His purposes for this dispensation and then comes back to take us into His presence, where we will hear that voice without any intervening medium of any sort. It will be the voice of God speaking directly to us, and we will understand it and know the voice of the Shepherd and look at His face, and His name will be on our foreheads.

A Christian who is confident in his or her faith is a result of the confirming work of the Holy Spirit through the Word of God. Out of this confirmation comes an authentic faith that brings the believer into harmony with the age's echo of the speaking voice of God.

## How Precious Is the Book Divine
John Fawcett (1740–1817)

How precious is the Book Divine,
By inspiration given!
Bright as a lamp its doctrines shine
To guide our souls to heaven.

It's light, descending from above
Our gloomy world to cheer,
Displays a Savior's boundless love
And brings his glories near.

It shows to man his wandering ways
And where his feet have trod,
And brings to view the matchless grace
Of a forgiving God.

O'er all the straight and narrow way
Its radiant beams are cast;
A light whose never weary ray
Grows brightest at the last.

It sweetly cheers our drooping hearts
In this dark vale of tears,
Life, light, and joy it still imparts
And quells our rising fears.

This lamp through all the tedious night
Of life shall guide our way
Till we behold the clearer light
Of an eternal day.

**Note**
1. Michael Bruce (1746–1767), "High the Heavenly Temple Stands."

# 3

# FAITH BEHOLDS THE FACE OF GOD

*For it became him, for whom are all things, and by whom are*
*all things, in bringing many sons unto glory, to make the captain*
*of their salvation perfect through sufferings.*

HEBREWS 2:10-13

God, being sovereign, answers to no man for His conduct and
will not stand before the bar of any human judgment. And yet,
God has made man a reasonable being, and it would not con-
form to man's reasoning mind to be always confronted with
unreasonable things. Therefore, God frequently shows His reasons for things, not because He, in His sovereignty, is answerable to you and to me, but because He chooses to give us some
answers, having honored us by making us in His image. So
Scripture says, "it became him." And He is going to show us
how it could be.

The great truth of Christ's incarnation, the condescension
of the second person of the Trinity, and the suffering of His
death, have to be justified before man's reason. Not that man
can ever make God answerable to him. That is beyond all
thought. God will answer to nobody. God is amenable to none.
Yet, God says, "All that I have done, it becomes me." It becomes

me is the old meaning of the word "becomes," meaning that what He has done is appropriate. It is the right thing.

It is the fit and becoming thing. I am perfectly happy to have God do things I cannot understand. I am joyfully willing that God should fly the plane for me, that He should run the machine for me, that He should portion out my life for me, that He should make my plans for me. I am perfectly willing that He should do all this, because He knows how, and I do not. He has the power, and I do not. However, being made in God's image, I have a mind that must know why a thing was done or at least know that it was not unreasonable.

## He Does All Things Well

It is necessary to my intellectual balance to understand that what God has done, He has done rightly. It is necessary to my moral health that I rise in the morning and know that however things come out, it will be all right. Either it will be good and favorable to me or it will be unfavorable. If good and favorable to me, then it will be by the grace of God. If unfavorable to me, it will be the discipline of God upon me. So either way, it will be all right.

The apostle Paul said, "But if I live in the flesh, this *is* the fruit of my labour: yet what I shall choose I wot not. For I am in a strait betwixt two, having a desire to depart, and to be with Christ; which is far better" (Phil. 1:22-23). We need to have that kind of faith and not depend on the things we see. We are never to lean on anything. When I see a man leaning against a building, it always makes me smile. I suppose he is resting himself, but the building does not need it, and he is wasting a lot of time there. We are not building on anything or trying to figure anything out. So I want to warn you away from trying to figure out the ways of God.

## Two Kinds of Christians

There are basically two types of Christians. There are those who are always telling you they have an "informed source." They say, "There's no news on this yet, but we have it from an informed source that they are going to do so-and-so." They imagine themselves in a position to have a private line to God's purposes. For example, when somebody falls down and breaks his leg, they immediately raise their eyebrow and say, "Uh-huh. I knew it. I knew that he had discipline coming." They did not know that at all. They are just mean little people who do not like the person and are glad he broke his leg. But they are pious enough that they want to find a good reason for that. Do not try that, because if the neighbor next door breaks his leg, and you say it was because he was not attending church or he did not tithe or he was not keeping up in prayer, what do you do when you break your leg? It would be a little bit embarrassing.

The other kind of Christian is the one that leaves everything to the Lord and does not try to figure out the ways of God because the ways of God are beyond finding out.

God sometimes honors us with reports to our intelligence, and says, "It becomes Me to do this. Do not worry about it; I am doing it the right way." I believe this. I live this way, and I believe God is doing it the right way. "Shall not the Judge of all the earth do right?" (Gen. 18:25) said Abraham. How did Abraham find that out?

If someone had said that in the seventeenth century or the twentieth century, he would have had several thousand years of biblical revelation behind him. He would have had all the preaching of the great preachers and the teaching of the great reformers. He would have had all the prophets, psalmists and Moses. He would have had the apostles, and he would have had the coming of Christ into the world. He would have had all that if he had spoken in the nineteenth or twentieth century. And rightly, we could have said, "He has figured that out." But it was Abraham who said it. And he did not have one line of written Scripture. He had never heard one hymn sung. He had never heard a sermon in his entire life. He had never been to a prayer meeting. He had never attended a conference where the Bible was taught. He had never been anywhere among the children of God. He had come from a heathen home in Ur of the Chaldees, and suddenly it burst upon him, "God has to do it right. The judge of the whole earth cannot be wrong." That belief became a strong pillar in the life of the man Abraham. We, today, must answer the question, "Shall not the judge of the whole earth do right?" with a radiant yes! The judge of the earth will do right.

## The Source of Most Evil

A basic truth of the Bible is that the source of most evil is a low opinion of God. In the book of Psalms, that truth comes out. "When thou sawest a thief, then thou consentedst with him, and hast been partaker with adulterers. Thou givest thy mouth to evil, and thy tongue frameth deceit. Thou sittest and speakest against thy brother; thou slanderest thine own mother's son. These things hast thou done, and I kept silence; thou thoughtest that I was altogether such an one as thyself: but I will reprove thee, and set them in order before thine eyes" (Ps. 50:18-21). We always try to make God in our image and pull Him down to our size. I am sure there are many deacons who conceive of God as a particularly large and very intelligent and good Deacon. They try to make God think like them.

It is not my business to try to make God think like me; it is my business to try to think like Him through prayer and meditation. For God made me in His image; I cannot make Him in mine. I have to remember God's treatment of the world and of the Church and of me, and I must have a blanket acceptance of God in these areas. I must say to my heart, "Do not try to edit God. Let God stand as He is. And whatever He does becomes Him. Whatever He does, that is right that He should do it. It is becoming of God that He should be that way. And do not try to change it."

When we remember that everything God does is going to be done in a perfectly wise manner, so there is no mistake possible, a wonderful peace of heart comes, along with growth and spiritual strength. He is perfectly just, so there is no unfairness possible. He is perfectly strong, so there is neither weakness nor failure possible. This we have to take as the basis upon which we build. Nobody builds on sand. You have to get down below the sand to the bedrock. The city of New York is built on one great piece of rock, one solid bedrock. To get down, they had to blast and chisel through rock. It is a good thing, because a high concentration of population with all those tall buildings towering into the sky would surely push down any weak foundation. You cannot push down a rock; and God is our rock.

These things about God are the rock upon which we stand. Salvation, then, is the infinitely wise plan of God carried through in perfect goodness with flawless precision to an infinitely efficacious consummation.

## God Works in Perfect Goodness

Allow me to break this down and simply say that God, being infinitely wise, has a plan for us. God is carrying out that plan in perfect goodness. There are no little bits of malice; everything is done in perfect goodness.

Someone once wrote an article about Christians and the exquisite malice of the people of God. I do not like that, and I wish it did not have to be said, but I do not suppose I have ever been anywhere where I have seen finer malice than in churches among Christian people. Christian people, however, have a way of disguising it.

Take a sinner. He will flip his cigarette into the gutter, curse you in great, rumbling loud noise and tell you in plain words where to go. Christians are too nice for that. A Christian would not be caught doing such an impossibly terrible thing. The Christian lowers his voice and in a pious tone skins him without his ever knowing his hide has been taken loose from his body. Christians have the most pious, perfect way, and everybody but God thinks we are fine people. We must get away from this.

Everything God does is perfectly good, and He does it flawlessly. There is, however, a consummation that is the end of all things. One of these days we are going to arrive at that.

## To Bring Many Sons to Glory

Notice in this Scripture that the effective operation of Christ's work is twofold: bringing sinners unto salvation and bringing sons unto glory. "Go ye therefore, and teach all nations, baptizing them in the name of the Father, and of the Son, and of the Holy Ghost: Teaching them to observe all things whatsoever I have commanded you: and, lo, I am with you always, even unto the end of the world. Amen" (Matt. 28:19-20). Our command is to go out into the world and make converts. That is, bring sinners to salvation. Then bring them into the church and instruct them, and that is helping to bring sons unto glory. God does it by His Word, by His discipline, by chastisement, by prayer and by fellowship with the saints. He does it in many ways to bring many sons unto glory.

When you were converted, you did not get a diploma saying, "This man, having met all requirements, is now being granted this diploma of salvation." It did not come that way. When you were converted, you were born again. You were a sinner made a Christian. You became a son or daughter, but you were not a completed son or daughter. You were not a finished son or daughter. You were just beginning, and the Lord took you there to lead you unto glory.

## Regeneration Is Only the Beginning

Many well-meaning Christians have developed what I shall call a distorted view about conversion. Many stress that nothing else matters; but regeneration is only the beginning of a new life, and wherever there is life, there is growth. Where there is no longer any growth, life begins to die out. As long as we are young and on our way up, we are growing. When we stop growing, we start down. Nobody likes to hear this. We like to think we are being renewed day by day. We are, in a measure; but in another measure, we are not. Regeneration is the beginning of a life, and sanctification is the development of that life, by the Holy Spirit, the blood, the Word, faith, prayer, discipline, hard work and by tribulation. We must be fed. Peter said we must as newborn babies take the sincere milk of the Word (see 1 Pet. 2:2).

I once put myself on a diet. Even though I do not believe in self-medication, I practice it all the time. I put myself on a diet of nothing but milk. None of this skinned-down skim milk; this was real Grade A. I drank six quarts a day. I thought I could do better if it was warm. Two quarts for breakfast, two for lunch and two for dinner. No dessert and nothing else. All this time I was preaching constantly and going to conventions and had them serve it to me at these places. Everywhere I went and even when I was home, two quarts of milk per meal. When it was all over, I had put on 15 pounds and never felt better in my life. I do not recommend this for others because some feel all right as it is and do not want to put on 15 pounds. Milk is a good food, and the Scripture says you are to take the sincere milk of the Word. And if you take it you will grow. Babies grow with milk, and this is why we are regenerated, that we might grow, with the purpose of bringing many sons unto glory.

## Ever Growing

Christians are not finished products; they are God's sons in process. The man looks at his year-old baby and thinks he is wonderful; but if he looks the same at three years old, the father worries about him. And if he looks the same at five years old, he knows something is tragically wrong. So when God looks at a new Christian and hears him saying, "Abba, Father," God is pleased. But after five years, if he has not got beyond "Abba, Father," I am sure the heart of God is concerned. If after 15 years of hanging around the church and only able to say, "Abba, Father," I am sure the Holy Spirit is grieved and heavy-hearted. God wants us to grow. He wants us to develop and mature. Not our size, but our maturity matters. So we are sons in process. We are buildings being put up; we are pictures being painted; we are sons growing to maturity.

## Tempted in All Things, Yet Without Sin

In order to do this, God made the Captain of our salvation perfect. These sons of God are an army led by a Captain, and the Leader of our salvation was made perfect through suffering. Now, you say, "Would the Lord Jesus Christ have to be perfected? Was He not born perfect? Was He not God of God and light of light? Was it not said of Him, 'That holy thing which shall be born of thee shall be called the Son of God' (Luke 1:35)?" Yes. He was all that, and more than we could ever say. But as a man, He had to be perfected.

What does that mean? It does not mean He had to be made morally perfect. When talking about us, it means that, but not when talking about Him. It means, completing His manhood. He had to be made perfect in the completion of manhood. A thing has to be tried. Nothing is good until it is tried. Nothing is perfect until it is tried. The child brought up in the nursery until he is 21 years old would not be perfect, even though through the wonders of science and proper diet and balance and air-conditioning he might be an example of all that is beautiful in manhood. He might be strong and healthy and vigorous, but he would be a long way from being a man. He would be a cream-puff. Imagine inducting him into the Army or Navy. He would die before midnight. You have to have more than simple growth; you have to have trials to bring you to perfection.

The oak tree that grows on the hill and withstands the storm year in and year out becomes tough. Its grain becomes deep and strong because it has the wind and the rain and the lightning and the tempest to perfect it.

So Jesus Christ, our Lord, who was pure to the point where He was holy and blameless and undefiled and separate from sinners, and higher than the highest heaven, could not have been the Christ if He had merely been a hothouse perfect man. He had to be more than that; He had to undergo all possible human experiences. The tempest had to break over Him the same as it did His disciples. The storms had to sweep down on Him. He had to be hungry; He had to suffer and be cursed as they were and be driven out as they were driven out. He had to be hated as they were hated; He had to walk until He was tired, and lie down and sleep. He had to rise in the morning and know the unpleasantness of getting going after a night's sleep. He had to know all that. He had to undergo it all. Nothing touched His brethren but He felt it. So there is a perfect kinship of experience with Jesus Christ, our Lord.

I have often wondered how kings, presidents and men in authority in high places who never came up the hard way understood their people. A man like Abraham Lincoln knew his people. But a man like John F. Kennedy, born with a silver spoon in his mouth, I do not know how he knew his people at all. How could he know? He did not know how a farm boy in Pennsylvania would do. But Jesus knew how His people did, because He was one of them. He was born in a stable, brought up in the carpenter shop and played with the little boys in the back lots. He helped His father when He got old enough; He listened to the preaching of John, was baptized, filled with the Holy Spirit and went out and labored among men; He slept under the trees at night and had nowhere to lay His head, and sometimes He hungered. He knew all about that. He knew a perfect kinship of experience with us.

Notice what it says: "For both he that sanctifieth and they who are sanctified are all of one: for which cause he is not ashamed to call them brethren" (Heb. 2:11). He is not ashamed to call them brethren. We are one with Him. Sometimes I like to kneel in reverent mood and remind myself that He is my brother at the right hand of God the Father.

Christ was made perfect through suffering. Some things you will never know until you have suffered. I wish I did not have to write this. I have an edgy feeling sometimes that I wish I did not always have to say the truth. It would be wonderful to quote nice things and tell people how good they are. People would congratulate me and say, "That was wonderful. I feel so much better." But the truth is, there are some things you cannot know until you suffer.

I want to say it now and say it bluntly: There are some imperfections you never lose until you have suffered. You will never know some truths until you have suffered either in your heart or in your body or both. And some mysteries, you will never understand until you have carried the cross and fallen under it. So we might as well brace ourselves for suffering.

Some imagine that Christianity is a playground. They are wrong. It is not a playground; it is a battleground. It is a field where men work and a battleground where men fight. It is along a highway where men walk, not ride. We might as well face up to that. But there is grace, thank God, plenty of grace. There is grace enough for everybody, and He never allows anybody to suffer or be tempted above what they are able to bear. With every temptation, He makes a way of escape. As long as there is a way of escape, we do not have to worry about the rest.

Remember, God is not ashamed to suffer. And He is not ashamed of you, and He is not ashamed of you when you are suffering. You sometimes may be ashamed of yourself. You might wince and whimper under it and feel ashamed, but He is not ashamed of you. He knows what you are going through. He went through it Himself. So God made the Captain of our salvation perfect through suffering.

"I have lived long and become an old man," said Mark Twain, "and I have suffered many things and had many troubles, most of which never came to pass." He was right about that. Most of our troubles do not happen. We suffer, fearing they will happen; therefore, we can cut down on the intensity of our fearing by not fearing. God will take those temptations and tribulations we suffer and purchase for us a crown of life. Though the devil is allowed to get to us, he is not allowed finally to harm us.

God is waiting now to bring sons unto the glory. Are you concerned to be a growing Christian? Are you concerned to be a maturing Christian? Do you know what it means to sing, "I long, oh, I long to be holy, conformed to His will and His Word. I want to be gentle and Christlike. I want to be just like my Lord"? Or, "Help me to be holy, O Father of light. Sin burdened and lowly, I bow in Thy sight. How can a stained conscience dare to look on Thy face? Even though in my presence Thou grant me a place"?

If I thought that even 20 percent of the professed church people were honestly longing to be holy, I would be a happy and gratified man. I hope I have underestimated it. I hope there are more who honestly want to be brought unto glory and are cooperating with Christ, seeking to know God, and willing to pay any price to know Him, to mount, to rise, to mature, to grow, to become strong. This ought to be the beating, yearning heart of the Church. "Oh, to be like thee, blessed Redeemer." That ought to be the watchword of the Church, for He is trying to bring sons unto the glory. And He will do it some way.

Let us cooperate with Him, so that the doing of it will cost us less time, less suffering and less trouble. For the more we cooperate, the less we have to suffer. But all of us will have to suffer in some measure. And this becomes God. So let us not blame God or complain. "Shall not a holy God do right?" He does right, and circumstances being what they are . . . and hell being what it is, and where it is . . . and we being who we are . . . and heaven being what it is . . . God is right in bringing many sons unto the glory through our perfect leader Jesus Christ, and us through suffering.

If we are to gaze into the face of God, we must look beyond our present circumstances. We must rest in the faithfulness of God and that all these things before us will work together for good. This is the faith that rises above all else and never stops short of a full gaze into the face of God. This is the place of our destined fellowship with God. Authentic faith rests fully in that gaze of the soul.

My looking for God must go beyond human reason, although it never contradicts reason. To know God is to trust Him completely. In order to seek God we must look beyond circumstances and in holy fascination gaze upon the one who loves us. The gaze of the soul is always toward God.

### Oh, to Be Like Thee
Thomas Obediah Chisholm (1866–1960)

O to be like Thee! Blessed Redeemer,
This is my constant longing and prayer;
Gladly I'll forfeit all of earth's treasures,
Jesus, Thy perfect likeness to wear.

O to be like Thee! full of compassion,
Loving, forgiving, tender and kind,
Helping the helpless, cheering the fainting,
Seeking the wandering sinner to find.

O to be like Thee! lowly in spirit,
Holy and harmless, patient and brave;
Meekly enduring cruel reproaches,
Willing to suffer others to save.

O to be like Thee! Lord, I am coming
Now to receive anointing divine;
All that I am and have I am bringing,
Lord, from this moment all shall be Thine.

O to be like Thee! while I am pleading,
Pour out Thy Spirit, fill with Thy love;
Make me a temple meet for Thy dwelling,
Fit me for life and Heaven above.

O to be like Thee! O to be like Thee,
Blessed Redeemer, pure as Thou art;
Come in Thy sweetness, come in Thy fullness;
Stamp Thine own image deep on my heart.

# 4

# OUR FAITH RESTS IN HIS LABORS

*There remaineth therefore a rest to the people of God. For he that is entered into his rest, he also hath ceased from his own works, as God did from his. Let us labour therefore to enter into that rest, lest any man fall after the same example of unbelief.*

HEBREWS 4:9-11

The quality of our Christian faith is in direct proportion to our resting in God, which is a result of totally embracing His finished work. Resting in God, outlined for us in Hebrews, consists of four types: a moral rest, a spiritual rest, an inward rest and the rest that satisfies. All aspects of this rest spring from the finished labor of Jesus. The majority of Christians frantically try to be what God wants them to be but will never be until they rest, that is, cease from their own labors and enter into His finished labor.

## Why We Can Rest

The Bible is very clear that no one has any right to rest until his work is done. "David, after he had served his own generation by the will of God, fell on sleep" (Acts 13:36). And the Lord labored until He could say, "I have finished the work which thou gavest me to do" (John 17:4). Rest follows labor, according to the will of God. According to man, rest and labor are so inter-mingled that the average person never gets tired. But in the Bible, this is not true. We labor; and when the labor is finished, we wash our hands and say, "Thank God that is done." Then we can properly sit down and rest.

The argument from Scripture for rest is that God wants us to finish the work and rest from it. That is shown in Genesis, speaking of the creation of all things. And He entered into His own rest after He had done the necessary work. That is, His rest was a cessation of labor, for you will notice that rest is a nega-tive thing, not a positive thing. I remember once that someone, hoping that he could help me, said, "Tozer, what you need is an intensive rest." I smiled about that. I can just see a man with his muscles tense and his knuckles white, intensely trying to rest. And we do that, but it is not true rest.

God entered into His rest, that is, He ceased from doing something. That is what rest is, the cessation of labor. Rest is automatic after that. When a work is to be done, no man has any right to rest until it is finished. Either the man has to do it or someone has to do it for him.

## The Role of Faith and Obedience

God offered Palestine to the Jews and said, "This is all yours, you will not need to plant a vineyard; it is all planted for you. You will not need to clear a field; all the fields are cleared and fenced. You will not have to start herds, for the herds are every-where. Milk and honey are flowing. The bees are there; the vines are bearing fruit. Everything is prepared for you. And I am driv-ing out the unworthy inhabitants who were unfit to live. And I

54

am going to turn this whole thing over to you free of charge. The work has already been done."

Israel refused and failed God all down the way. In unbelief, they refused, and forfeited their rest. So after all these years, the book of Hebrews was written arguing from this history of Israel. There was a rest that could have been the possession of the Jews. They could have had it. It was theirs. God was offering them Palestine because a work had already been done and all they had to do was move in, unpack their things and settle down. The rest was theirs by the labor of others. Israel met this offer in unbelief and never occupied all of the land. They were in and out of the land, and sometimes in bondage to the people of the land. They never quite had the faith or the obedience to go in, take over the land and enter into God's rest.

## Why Rest Eludes Man

Hebrews goes on to say that there is another rest offered to us in the gospel. And this is not a rest by already having herds of cattle and houses already built and fountains already flowing and orchards already bearing fruit. This is a spiritual rest of which the others—for example, the Israelites entering into the Promised Land—were merely symbolic. This is a rest of the heart. This is the rest of the question, "What am I going to do about sin?" It has to do with holiness, and, "How am I going to face the great God Almighty in that day to come? How am I going to stand up there in that awful judgment day, before the blazing throne, with sin on my heart? How am I going to satisfy justice, which demands that I should die for my sins? How am I going to pay my moral debt? I am a man under deep debt."

If you were in debt to the government for unpaid income tax, you would be properly worried. Yet, if somebody came along and said, "Here, you owe $10,000 in back taxes, and the government is breathing down your neck; I will take care of it for you. I will pay your debt. Here is the receipt." You certainly would rest, wouldn't you? You would relax for the first time and sleep well at night. You would say, "I am not worried when I see a police officer anymore. I am not thinking he is after me. He is just walking down the street, looking for criminals, and I am all right. I have earned rest of mind; I have entered into my rest. Not mine, but the rest of another." That is exactly what the Bible teaches here.

The Christian's rest is based upon the work of another. It is not his own work, for that he could never do. It is the work of another, who is capable of earning that rest, capable of procuring it. The Christian is not capable; nobody is capable. You and I cannot deal with the matter of holiness outraged. We cannot deal with a matter of justice violated. We cannot take care of the question of sins committed and a moral debt. We cannot, and it is impossible that we should, for the best we could possibly do is to stop sinning now and not add any more to the debt. But we cannot pay one penny on the debt we already owe. The debt we already owe is so great that it would send us into hell. So now we have to pay that before we can rest. We owe a debt we cannot pay, not to a government but to God Almighty, to the eternal God. When the conviction of that truth strikes dead center, we call it "getting under conviction."

I believe the Bible is clear in stating that we cannot pay our own debt. The best that we can do is pay from here forward, but we could not even do that until all the back taxes still owing are paid. What happens then? There is someone who comes and lays down His life, the just for the unjust, who pays the debt that He did not owe and includes in that debt all of our debts. He propitiates for violated holiness; He atones for justice that is broken. He does all of this. He is capable of it. And the whole book of Hebrews argues for the capability of Jesus, that He is able to do it. It is one thing to make a promise, but it is quite another thing to be able to carry it out. And Jesus has done just that.

Our Lord Jesus came and said, "Lo, I come (in the volume of the book it is written of me,) to do thy will, O God" (Heb. 10:7). Was He able to do it? The book of Hebrews declares loudly and logically that He was able to do it. "He had by himself purged our sins, sat down on the right hand of the Majesty on high" (Heb. 1:3).

The vital question is, "If you will hear His voice?" Shall we be like Israel in those days when they heard the gospel, the good news, that there was a place for them in which they did not have to cut down the tree or blow out a stump or clear a field? It was all theirs. They did not have faith to believe it, and so they never enjoyed it. They entered in, but it was always under a shadow, and they never got it all. Shall we be like them and so fail completely? Or shall we do our own labor and enter into our own rest? For any man who knows his own heart would not dare to stand and say, "I am morally capable of earning my own rest." You would put that man down as being a moral fool. For a man who knows his own heart knows better. We either have to satisfy God's holiness, satisfy His violated justice and pay the moral debt, or we have to have somebody do it for us. The book of Hebrews declares that somebody did it for us. The eternal Son did that work.

## Looking for Rest in All the Wrong Places

Many people do not want this kind of rest. They want another kind. Those who want a moral rest want to know what it is to rest from the yearning for character.

From the time I was a boy, I have heard an expression I never liked: "character building." The liberal theologians use it a lot, as well as educators. They are building character. I suppose it is all right, really. I guess I would have to admit it is a valid phrase. But you usually like or dislike a phrase because of the context in which you heard it. I used to hear it uttered by men I knew did not know what they were talking about. Therefore, "character building" does not please me too well.

You cannot build character. You can take a man dying of cancer and teach him to speak and read Greek and Hebrew and Latin; to sing opera; to enjoy great music and art; but he is still a dying man, and you are not building anything in him. He is a dying man.

You can take a sinner and teach him to be an honest and square shooter, make him into a good citizen. There is no question that you can help a man. Our schools can help the character of our children. We ought to stand in silent salute to the teachers that have helped train our young people—who have taught them that it is better to be good than bad. That it is better to be honest than crooked. That it is better to tell the truth than to lie. I think we ought to thank God for the teachers. But it is only teaching a dying man to speak good English, making a cultured man out of a dying man. He and his culture are going to die together. That is what character building is. That is all it is. It is better than nothing, but it is not enough.

Many people are anxious to do meritorious deeds, which is good. When I was a young person in my teens, I dreamed of going to war and coming home a hero. When I would hear "The Star-Spangled Banner," I would get goose bumps and say, "Oh, I would just love to go out and die for something and come back." I wanted to die for my country, and then I wanted to come back and enjoy it. But it does not work out that way. I never got any higher than a buck private when I was in the service, never had a gun in my hand, so I rather fizzled out on that one. But we all want to do meritorious deeds. We want to go out and do something big. When we come to think of God and the things of the carnal world, we want to do virtuous deeds. We want to be known as a virtuous person.

Benjamin Franklin was so eager to be a good man that he made a sheet of paper divided into squares like a tight checkerboard and had "Monday, Tuesday . . ." all of the days of the week written on it. He had the virtues on the left-hand side: honesty, modesty, humility and truth. Then each day he would go down that list and check where he had failed. If there was a blank spot, that meant he had been all right. But if he failed, he checked it off. He wanted to be good, and I thank God for everybody who wants to be good rather than give up and sink into the mud. But that still is not enough. Benjamin Franklin never found rest.

Building character never accomplishes any kind of rest, because you are never done building. You never find rest when you are only seeking to do virtuous deeds. In the warfare of the flesh and the spirit, we can only be delivered in that warfare, and we can only win if we take deliverance by resting.

## The Eternal Son's Finished Work

The Holy Spirit says, "Let us therefore fear, lest, a promise being left us entering into his rest, any of you should seem to come short of it" (Heb. 4:1). The promise still holds good. But, you say, didn't Joshua lead them in?

The argument is that if Joshua had led the Israelites in and they had obtained that rest, then why should God, centuries later, say, "If ye will hear his voice, harden not your hearts" (Heb. 3:15)? Joshua could not give rest to Israel because of Israel's unbelief. But there is a rest spoken of by David, centuries after Joshua. He says it is an inward rest. It is a rest of the soul. It is a rest from our labor. The promise still holds good. We are to attain God's rest.

Some may have missed this chance. Many have fooled with religion, played with Christianity, been in and out of churches, heard this and that speaker, read this book and that book, but they did it all in unbelief. Our unbelief has blocked any effort of the Spirit to lead us into rest. We develop mental habits. They get fixed in our hearts; we get tough and unresponsive. When that happens, we should plow deep, break up our fallow ground and seek to be able to respond quickly, to be responsive and sensitive to the voice of God calling us to cease from our labors and trust in Jesus Christ completely, wholly, that we might be able to rest from our struggles. Most Christians are not very restful about this matter.

I heard a Methodist bishop once say that he had found, as a pastor, that 70 percent of his parishioners were not ready for heaven. They had to cram for the examination at the last minute before they felt free to get in. They were not resting in what Christ had done. They were vaguely hoping about what they might do or had done. Somebody heard the bishop and said, "Bishop, are you not a bit rough there when you said 70 percent? Is that right?"

He said, "I am telling you the truth. It's 70 percent." Then he said, "I counted them. Only about 30 percent of my parishioners were ready to go."

More than two-thirds of those who went to church for a lifetime sang the hymns of Zion, heard the Scriptures read, listened to prayers and engaged in them and heard great preaching (for there were great preachers in those days). But when they came to die, they had not entered into rest. They could not go without fear.

I want God to lead me to a place where there is no fear in dying because I am resting in God, resting in what Jesus Christ has done for me. God did His work and entered into His rest. His Son Jesus Christ did another work, and we enter into that rest. Let us see that we do it. Let us search ourselves before God.

When I rest wholly and completely in Jesus Christ and His finished work, faith leaps up and alleviates from me the frantic labor of trying to make it. I rest perfectly and securely in the labor of Jesus Christ.

# O That My Load of Sin Were Gone!
Charles Wesley (1707–1788)

O that my load of sin were gone!
O that I could at last submit
At Jesus' feet to lay it down,
To lay my soul at Jesus' feet!

Rest for my soul I long to find:
Savior of all, if mine Thou art,
Give me Thy meek and lowly mind,
And stamp Thine image on my heart.

Break off the yoke of inbred sin,
And fully set my spirit free:
I cannot rest till pure within,
Till I am wholly lost in Thee.

Fain I would learn of Thee, my God;
Thy light and easy burden prove,
The cross, all stained with hallowed blood,
The labor of Thy dying love.

I would, but Thou must give the power;
My heart from every sin release;
Bring near, bring near the joyful hour,
And fill me with Thy perfect peace.

# FAITH LEADS TOWARD SPIRITUAL PERFECTION

*Therefore leaving the principles of the doctrine of Christ,*
*let us go on unto perfection.*

HEBREWS 6:1

Even the casual student of scriptural truth will conclude that God continually urges His people on to perfection. Although our faith comes from resting in the finished work of Christ, it never allows us to rest short of perfection. The great problems facing contemporary Christians is the fact that many are in a state of what I call arrested development. That is, they have grown to a certain point and then for whatever reason, there is no more growth. Many things contribute to this spiritual atrophy, and happy is the Christian who deals with these things.

## What Perfection Is Not

Perhaps the first question that comes to the surface is what is meant by spiritual perfection. If we are to go on "unto perfection," what is that perfection, and how am I going to know when I get there? The definitive answer to this would go a long way in solving a host of problems for the Christian in his daily walk. Many Christians have suffered unduly because of misunderstanding and a lack of teaching in this area.

Just as a newborn baby is not fully prepared to face the world, so too the newborn Christian is not fully prepared. There must be growth leading to a full-fledged maturity, which is another way of saying perfection. Perfection does not mean, as some have thought it to mean, sinless perfection. Rather, it is maturity as God intended. A baby is not born to stay a baby, but rather to grow into a mature adult.

In order to understand what is meant by spiritual perfection, I need to begin with several things that it is not. I have already mentioned that it is not coming to a point of sinless perfection. But in another sense, I can sum it all up into one statement that spiritual maturity, or perfection, has absolutely nothing to do with man's idea of perfection. Unfortunately, this is what we are getting in popular Christianity today.

Sinless perfection is not the best of man pushed to its ultimate height. No matter how you polish man, he always falls short of God's idea of perfection.

Man's idea of perfection separates into three different categories: the natural man, the moral man and the religious man.

## The Natural Man

So many examples of the natural man abound. Just about at every level, we find endeavors in perfecting the natural man to his ultimate height. Yet, in spite of all of the polishing that goes on, there is a depraved aspect of humanity that cannot be obliterated.

Spiritual perfection is not the perfection of the natural man. The natural man is that man as he is without Jesus Christ. It is man as the result of the Fall in the Garden of Eden, which can never be brought to a point of spiritual perfection. When God told Adam and Eve that if they ate of that fruit in the garden they would die, they died spiritually, leaving the natural man deprived of any spiritual life.

The natural man boasts in himself. You cannot read a magazine today without seeing this, and it has even seeped into Christian magazines. Perfection in this regard is being the best you can possibly be, but it is always short of what God desires. There is something deep within the heart of every man and woman, a yearning for that which is beyond themselves. Unfortunately, in the natural there is no way to define that "beyond," never mind trying to reach it. In every advancement in the human race is the strain to become what it was created to be; every generation falls short of that expectation. Perfection is not what we can be or what we can achieve, but what God created us for initially.

Even, perchance, we could bring the natural man to a point of perfection, it would still be far short of what the Bible calls "the glory of God." The natural man at his best falls short of understanding what that hidden yearning, the deep that calleth unto deep, is all about. Everything is focused upon himself and his interests and his concerns and what pleases him. And all of these things fall short of that deep satisfaction that man is capable of enjoying.

The genius of man expressed in all the inventions from time immemorial only shows a deep-seated dissatisfaction within the heart of man—always trying to improve, but always falling short. What one generation succeeds in doing, the next generation has no tolerance for. Each generation reinvents itself because of the deep inner yearning that cannot be satisfied with outward things.

The natural man is not able to experience the fulfillment of the pleasure he was created to enjoy. Even though the natural man is committed to the pursuit of pleasure, nothing he finds satisfies him. Therefore, he fills his life with what the Bible calls "the world, the flesh and the devil." His life has become a sham shrouded in unfulfilled expectations.

The perfection of the natural man falls short of anything resembling spiritual perfection.

## The Moral Man

Certainly there is something to be said for striving for good morals. Personally, I would rather live next to a man who exercises good morals than someone who does not. But the pursuit of good morals is not quite enough. For example, what is the standard used for defining good morals? In the book of Judges, we find a phrase that really defines this present generation: "In those days there was no king in Israel: every man did that which was right in his own eyes" (Judg. 21:25). In other words, everyone had his or her own definition of what is right.

The Ten Commandments were the epitome of moral perfection. But they fell short of God's ideal of perfection.

You might remember Jesus discussing this with the Pharisees of His day. In Matthew 5:27-28, Jesus shot down moral perfection as they understood it: "Ye have heard that it was said by them of old time, Thou shalt not commit adultery: But I say unto you, that whosoever looketh on a woman to lust after her hath committed adultery with her already in his heart."

The Pharisees took great pride in keeping the outside clean, but they gave no regard to the heart. It is the interior of the man that can never be reached or controlled by a mere law or commandment.

In other places, Jesus referred to the Pharisees as "whited sepulchres" because of their hypocrisy. "Woe unto you, scribes and Pharisees, hypocrites! for ye are like unto whited sepulchres, which indeed appear beautiful outward, but are within full of dead men's bones, and of all uncleanness" (Matt. 23:27). A person can achieve a place of moral perfection, externally speaking, but be inwardly rotten to the core. This was Jesus' contention with the Pharisees.

## The Religious Man

Religion is a composite of doing good works so that you can earn something. Some have the idea that the perfection of good works will lead to a satisfying life. If you just do the right thing for the right motive, you will have a very satisfying life. Every religion in the world is devoted to this kind of thing.

But here there is no perfection. The rich young ruler who came to Jesus was a man who had perfected his good works throughout his life. His question to Jesus is most disturbing: "The young man saith unto him, All these things have I kept from my youth up: what lack I yet?" (Matt. 19:20).

Imagine, a man like him coming to a point in his life, after doing everything he possibly could to lead a good life, and saying, "What lack I yet?" I cannot think of anything more dis-couraging—a man who does all the right things for all the right reasons and still feels an emptiness inside that nothing has been able to touch. Even he knew, in the midst of all his good works and keeping the law and perfecting his moral life, that some-thing was lacking in his life.

If there was one thing Jesus stood against during His public ministry, it was the emptiness of religious perfection. A person could go through all of the rites of religion, give all the sacrifices required of the law, keep every holy day in the books and still be empty inside. "What lack I yet?"

The natural man, the moral man and the religious man all share one thing: They all pursue a pseudo-fulfillment of life expressed in greed and selfishness, harboring within themselves yearnings that cannot be explained or satisfied. Their best exists through positive thinking, psychology, education and everything that has to do with the outward person. All of these things polish the outside yet conceal the fact that the inside is filthy to the core.

This idea of perfection can be boiled down to one phrase, "be-ing the best you can possibly be." This falls short of the undiscov-ered potential in every human being put there by God, the Creator. He did not create us to be the best we can be apart from Himself. When you eliminate God from your life, you greatly undercut your created potential.

## Back to Our Original Purpose

What do we mean when we talk about spiritual perfection? If the natural man, the moral man and the religious man fall short of all of this, what else is there?

Allow me to outline for you what I mean by spiritual perfection. Spiritual perfection has to do with God's ultimate purpose for humanity. This purpose has not changed since the
very beginning of creation. God created Adam and Eve in the
Garden for the same purpose.

In order to understand this we have to keep two things in
mind.

First, why did God create Adam and Eve? What was the
purpose behind their creation?

For this, we need to go back to Genesis and discover how it
all began. There is something in Bible study called the "law of
first mention." This is a very important law enabling us to understand what the Scripture has to say in its totality. It simply
means that when the Scriptures first mention something, it es-
tablishes a pattern with that subject that remains unchanged in
the mind of God throughout Scripture.

In Genesis, we discover God's purpose for humanity: "And
God said, Let us make man in our image, after our likeness:
and let them have dominion over the fish of the sea, and over
the fowl of the air, and over the cattle, and over all the earth,
and over every creeping thing that creepeth upon the earth"
(Gen. 1:26).

Whatever else that may mean, it means that man was originally created for God and for fellowship with God. Unlike any
other of God's creations, only man has fellowship with God.
God walked in the cool of the day in the Garden only with
Adam and Eve. We never find Him walking in the cool of the
day with an elephant or a tiger or a guerrilla. Only man was created "after our likeness."

What brought that to an end was the fall of man, in the Garden. Man fell because of the deceitfulness of Satan, and the resulting horrific sin destroyed within man that fellowship for which he was created, leaving a void within.

Second, we come to the New Testament and to the cross of Christ. It was the purpose of redemption to bring man back to his original purpose—back to that place of full fellowship with God. Redemption was not designed just to make us better people. Redemption was not to help make us the best we could possibly be in the flesh. Redemption has a spiritual component to it, our connection to the Godhead and rediscovering our intended purpose.

So God's ultimate purpose for mankind was to enjoy unlimited fellowship and intimacy. This fellowship is not a stagnant, passive thing. Rather, it is dynamic and growing. The end result is that we would be more and more like Jesus Christ.

Man's ideal of perfection always excludes Christ. But God's idea of perfection is complete maturity in Jesus Christ. The hymn writer said, "O, to be like Thee."

Man's idea of perfection is to reach man's highest ideal. God's idea of perfection is for us to reach our highest ideal in Christ.

I have always appreciated St. Augustine's opening chapter in his revealing book, *Confessions of St. Augustine*. In that opening chapter, he says, "Thou hast created us for Thyself and we are restless until we rest fully in Thee." This is the impetus behind spiritual perfection from a biblical viewpoint. We have been created for a purpose, and until that purpose is satisfied and fulfilled, we have a restlessness about us that cannot be satiated by any other thing in this world. It is so deep within us that nothing human or natural can touch it.

God looks at us through the Lord Jesus Christ. When He looks at us, He is anticipating Christ in all of His fullness and glory. This is the spiritual perfection of which the Bible speaks. This is what is meant by going on to full maturity in Christ.

## Revealing the Image of Christ

I once read of a great sculptor whose sculptures were prized by everyone. Someone once asked him the secret of his masterpieces. He said something to the effect, "I just chip away everything that doesn't belong there." That sculptor looked at the lump of granite or whatever and saw something in it nobody else saw. The genius of his masterpiece was to eliminate everything that did not belong there and allow the vision of that image to emerge.

God created man for Himself, to have sweet, intimate fellowship with Him on a daily and growing basis. When He looks at man through the cross of the Lord Jesus Christ, He sees what nobody else can see. He sees Christ. Everything in that man's life that does not belong there, everything that is not Christ, He painstakingly begins to remove. He may take months or years to finish His masterpiece. However, He is in no hurry because of the delicate nature of His work and the ultimate result of His craftsmanship.

And so, God, in no hurry whatsoever, painstakingly chips away, removing everything that is not part of the image of Christ. He takes the initiative to interrupt our lives for the higher cost of developing us into spiritually mature believers.

What if a master sculptor was working on a piece of granite, and the granite objected to the many chips falling to the floor? What if that piece of granite began dictating to the master where and what he should chip away? That kind of thing is incomprehensible. And so it is with us. God is the great Master Architect and Sculptor of that image of Christ within us. He knows what He is doing, but often it seems to us that He has taken away a few chips too many.

Sometimes we feel that the Master has gone too far. Be assured, the divine Master Craftsman knows exactly what He is doing, because He has an ultimate goal in mind. One thing we need to get hold of is the fact that this world is not the end. We are too quick to live this life and forget there is a world to come.

The old preachers of another generation used to talk about the fact that this life was preparation for the life to come. We do not hear that much anymore. We are listening to the voices of the natural man and the moral man and the religious man whose focus is all on this life and never on the world to come. But the thing that the Master Architect and Sculptor is doing in my life is preparing me, not so much for this world, but for the world to come.

The great hymn writer Fanny J. Crosby understood this and expressed it in many of her hymns. Her hymn "Saved by Grace" says:

> Someday my earthly house will fall
> I cannot tell how soon 'twill be;
> But this I know—my All in All
> Has now a place in heaven for me.

Her focus was not on the earthly house. She knew one day it would decay and fall away. Her hope was in her "All in All," who is none other than Jesus Christ. He was the Great Architect and Sculptor of her life. He was the one designing her life not for this world but for the world to come.

God's primary intention for every believer is for him or her to "go on unto perfection" (Heb. 6:1). In this regard, God will stop short of nothing to accomplish this end. If need be, God will interrupt your life in any way imaginable without asking your permission. Your spiritual perfection rests in the wisdom of Him who has created you in His image.

## Gently Lead Us
Thomas Hastings (1784–1872)

Gently, Lord, oh, gently lead us
Through vale of tears,
Though thou'st decreed us,
Till our last great change appears.

As temptation's darts assail us,
Or in devious paths we stray
Let thy goodness never fail us,
Lead us in thy perfect way

In the hour of pain and anguish,
In the hour when death draws near
Suffer not our hearts to languish,
Suffer not our souls to fear.

As this mortal life is ended,
Bid us in thine arms to rest,
Till, by angel bands attended,
We awake among the blest.

Then, oh, crown us with thy blessing,
Through the triumphs of thy grace;
Then shall praises never ceasing
Echo through thy dwelling-place.

6

# FAITH RISES ABOVE THE TWISTS AND TURNS OF LIFE

*But, beloved, we are persuaded better things of you,*
*and things that accompany salvation, though we thus speak.*
HEBREWS 6:9

It always amazes me how some people can take a subject like faith and spin it to accommodate their personal agenda. No matter what your problem is, the solution is faith. If you need more money, take it by faith. If you want an advancement in your career, claim it by faith and you will get it for sure. The motto of many is, "Just believe it and you will receive it." Or, "Name it and claim it."

For some reason, they bypass what Hebrews says here: "We are persuaded better things of you." To use faith as a vehicle to get what you want is certainly not the "better things" spoken of here. I think that of all the books in the Bible, Hebrews suffers more from this kind of thing than any other book.

Whenever I hear a man preach along this line or pick up a book that addresses the subject, I immediately think of the sign I saw above a small factory. The factory specialized in all kinds of things made out of wood. Clothespins, wooden chair legs and everything you might imagine. The sign out front said this, "All Kinds of Twisting and Turning Done Here." The sign could be put on many books written about faith.

I will acknowledge that the sixth chapter of Hebrews is perhaps one of the most difficult chapters in the Bible. Therefore, it is inevitable that when it is the subject of sermons, all kinds of twisting and turning come from preachers who do not know what they are talking about. The preacher has a well-established theological position, and from that point, he tries to filter the Bible through that theological template. It is possible to push a square peg into a round hole, but in so doing you will destroy the square peg. The only question that seems to come to mind to many of these theologians today is, "Does this fit into my theological position?" And if it does not fit, they have all sorts of ways to throw it to the side disingenuously. Many are masters at this twisting and turning to bring Scripture into harmony with some preconceived idea they might have.

If we take Hebrews 6 in context, it begins to unfold itself for us. I firmly believe that nothing in the Bible has to be twisted and turned to fit into some theological position.

Now, I believe in theology. Theology is simply the study of God. What could be more important or exciting than that? But a form of theology that excludes aspects of the Bible is not a theology that can be trusted.

Along these lines, I have often said that Christians do not tell lies; they just go to church and sing them. It amazes me to see how many people will sing a hymn that does not really fit into their doctrinal bias. Perhaps many Christians have no idea of what they are singing when they sing a hymn. And preachers are the worst ones along this line. I have been in meetings where right after singing one of the grand old hymns of the Church, the preacher will step to the pulpit and ruin the whole thing by preaching a sermon absolutely contrary to the doctrine expressed in that hymn. The sad part is that most of them do not know they are doing this. This may explain why there is such a decline in singing of hymns in churches today.

Biblical faith, as outlined in the Scriptures, and particularly in the book of Hebrews, challenges us to rise above all of the twists and turns that we may find within the Church. It does not honor God for us to take the Scriptures and try to make them mean something God did not mean originally. Let me lay out an example.

## A Man-Created Doctrinal Fence

I am often asked if I am a Calvinist or an Arminian. For many people this is a very crucial question, and they need to know which side of the old doctrinal fence you are on. The pressure has come to such a point that everybody has to choose which way they are going to go. Are you going to be a Calvinist, or are you going to be an Arminian? If you are Calvinist, you certainly cannot go along with anything Arminian. And, if you are an Arminian, there is no way that you can stomach anything Calvinistic.

I think the whole thing is rather dangerous. It would be like somebody asking you to choose between your right hand and your left hand. If you use your right hand, then you have to get rid of that left hand. Now, what kind of nonsense would that be? I have a right hand and a left hand, and they work very nicely together.

When somebody approaches the subject with me, I often think about a famous English preacher who said, "When I preach, I'm an Arminian. When I pray, I'm a Calvinist." I have always appreciated that answer and believe it most correctly defines me and many other good solid evangelicals. I think this preacher was saying that he was an equivocating Calvinist and an apologetic Arminian. My question is, what were people before John Calvin was born? Why can't we just be Christians?

I serve on the Christian and Missionary Alliance mission board, and have done so for many years. Serving on the board with me are two of my best friends. We go back a long way, all three of us. We have come by different paths, but we have become good friends down through the years. One of them is a staunch Calvinist. If you would go to his church on Sunday, you would feast on a wonderful Calvinistic sermon. The other friend is Arminian—a staunch Arminian at that. If you would go to his church on any given Sunday, you would feast on an Arminian banquet such as you have never had before.

Even though these two friends come from different positions doctrinally, when we meet on that mission board, we are in complete harmony. Both leave their doctrinal biases at the door and join hearts, seeking the mind of the Lord for our mission board.

Now that is what I mean. When we allow doctrinal biases to determine whom we can fellowship with, we are guilty of twisting and turning the Scriptures. This does not have to be.

I can go down through Church history and find great Christians on both sides of this issue. This leads me to believe that it must not be a very important issue. I do not think you have to choose between being a Calvinist and an Arminian. If so, then one side is wrong. Now, which side is going to be wrong?

I have one example in mind, and it has to do with John Wesley. Wesley, the founder of the Methodist church, was a staunch, dyed-in-the-wool Arminian. He had no time for any of the Calvinistic nonsense, as he called it. I read some of his sermons, and he was an Arminian all right.

That is not the end of the story. At John Wesley's deathbed, his family and friends were gathered around him. They heard him singing something very faintly. One of the family bent over to try to hear what he was singing. He was singing a hymn. As they leaned closer to hear, what do you suppose he was singing?

> I'll praise my Maker while I've breath,
> And when my voice is lost in death,
> Praise shall employ my nobler powers;
> My days of praise shall ne'er be past,
> While life, and thought, and being last,
> Or immortality endures.

Who do you suppose wrote that hymn? None other than Isaac Watts (1674–1748), who was a staunch Calvinist. And so, this staunch Arminian closed out the last moments of his life, heart in heart with a Calvinist, singing, "I'll praise my Maker while I've breath." When it comes to worship and adoring our Maker, there is no such thing as a Calvinist or an Arminian. Such distinctions fall away from the heart beating in worship.

I have it on good information that there will be no such distinctions in heaven as Calvinists or Arminians. Such things are not allowed beyond the pearly gates. Friends of mine from Pennsylvania often tease me when I am there by saying there will be no denominations in heaven but one. That one denomination will be Brethren in Christ. It is hard to argue with that.

If the preacher is a Calvinist, you will find a lot of twisting and turning in his preaching. The same goes for an Arminian. My question is, why don't we rise above all of this twisting and turning in trying to make the Scriptures support our doctrinal position? Why don't we just believe the Bible?

I believe that faith in Jesus Christ is of such a nature that it enables us to rise above all the pettiness we find around us.

## Classic Doctrinal Twists and Turns

Now, what about Hebrews 6? When we come to that chapter, there are all kinds of twisting and turning done by preachers. Let me point out a few.

### "Once Enlightened"

Many will say that "once enlightened" means they merely had light. They were not actually born-again people, but simply had light. But I like to compare Scripture with Scripture. I think that is the only way to do it. And in the Scriptures I find the same word is used by the apostle Paul in Ephesians 1:18-19: "The eyes of your understanding being enlightened; that ye may know what is the hope of his calling, and what the riches of the glory of his inheritance in the saints, and what is the exceeding greatness of his power to us-ward who believe, according to the working of his mighty power." The same word "enlightened" is used in both places.

It takes a lot of twisting and turning to make it mean one thing in one verse and another thing in another verse. In Ephesians, the apostle Paul was praying that the Christians would grow in their spiritual life. They were Christians. They did not just have light, but were enlightened by the work of the Holy Spirit within their hearts. Now, if it means this in Ephesians, the same word must mean the same thing in Hebrews.

## "Tasted of the Heavenly Gift"

Here is where the twisters and turners begin to work feverishly, insisting that they merely tasted it but never actually experienced the heavenly gift. They were not Christians, just people who nibbled at the truth and then turned away.

But I find that same word, "tasted," used in Hebrews 2:9: "But we see Jesus, who was made a little lower than the angels for the suffering of death, crowned with glory and honour; that he by the grace of God should taste death for every man." What I want to know is, are these twisters and turners prepared to suggest that Jesus only nibbled at death? That Jesus did not really experience death, but merely nibbled at it? I think this is heresy of the first order.

## "Made Partakers of the Holy Ghost"

Here is another phrase susceptible to the twisting and turning. The word "partakers" is twisted into meaning they just went along for the ride. They were not really committed to it. However, elsewhere this word is used to mean "be a participant in, to take part in, and to accept, and to eat and receive." I find it difficult to come away from this word without understanding that it means "experience." They had received and experienced the Holy Spirit.

## "It Is Impossible for Those Who Were Once Enlightened"

This one phrase gets more twisting and turning than any of the rest. Christians who had what Paul prayed the Ephesians might have, and have tasted of the heavenly gift—that is, "experienced" the heavenly gift and were made partakers, that is to take part in the Holy Spirit, and have experienced the good word of the Lord and the powers to come—if they shall fall away, it is impossible to renew them. Evidently, there is somebody the writer was thinking of that you and I cannot renew. It is impossible for us to renew him to repentance when this has happened.

The difficulty lies in two phrases: "fall away" and "renew unto repentance." And right here is where the twisting and turning gets a little crazy. What does the Scripture mean by "fall away"? And just how far does a person fall? Is this talking about backsliding? Well, if it is, then I see several difficulties. Two of the outstanding backsliders in the New Testament were Peter and John Mark. The Scriptures tell us that both of these men backslid but then repented, were forgiven and came back into full fellowship (see Mark 14:66-72; Acts 15:36-41). Peter's sermon on the Day of Pentecost gave birth to the Church. After Mark's repentance, Paul found him quite useful for the ministry. So, I have a difficult time seeing this "fall away" to be backsliding.

According to some of these twisters and turners, it is impossible to renew these people unto repentance. Certainly, this is not what Hebrews is talking about at all. It is possible to be so bogged down with doctrinal minutia that we lose all sense of what God is trying to say to us.

Let me give you a little rule here that might prove helpful. I am sure this rule will hold throughout the whole church of God around the world, for all time. *If you worry about committing the unpardonable sin, you have not committed it.* The person who has gone so far in apostasy that there is no hope for him never worries about it. In Matthew 12:3, the Pharisees gave vent to certain words, which Christ branded as evidence of the unpardonable sin. Yet, these Pharisees were not the slightest bit worried about it. They believed themselves to be righteous. There was no penitence in them, no compunction, no sorrow, no repentance, no humility and no meekness. They were bold believers in their own righteousness. Jesus said they had committed the unpardonable sin in that they had attributed the work of the Holy Spirit to the devil. So, if they had feared they had committed it, they would have been humble, lowly, meek, frightened and would have come like the jailer, shaking and trembling, and saying, "Lord, what must I do to be saved?" But they had no thought of this at all.

So, if you are worrying about having committed the unpardonable sin, you have not. The very fact that you are worried about it indicates the Spirit of God is moving in your heart; the Spirit of God does not move in the heart of a man who has committed "a sin unto death." I do not even know if "falling away" is the sin unto death. If we only knew what "fall away" meant. It must mean something that goes so far that the man does not care about it, does not worry about it, has no further feeling concerning it and shrugs it off as a foolish thing.

Here I am, back where I started, an equivocating Calvinist and an apologetic Arminian. Some believe you can be born again, then sin and be lost. Others take the other side and deny this, explain it and interpret it away. It is possible to fall off both ends of the log.

A young woman once said to me, "I have been saved three times." Certainly, I do not like to hear that, nor do I accept it. Obviously, this young woman had no concept of what it means to be saved. Then, of course, neither do we want to come out on the other side and say as some people do, "I am converted, and I couldn't go to hell if I wanted to." Personally, I would be a little afraid of that. In fact, I hardly think anybody who would ever say anything like that was converted in the first place; our faith is not so much what we believe but in whom we believe. And all the twisting and turning in the world cannot change this basic biblical truth.

## The Fallout of Twisted Biblical Truth

All of this twisting and turning carries with it some serious spiritual dangers. And to be honest, we all are guilty of this to some measure, at some time in our life. I think it is important to understand the dangers associated with all of this twisting and turning. Let me share with you a few that I see.

### It Promotes Trusting in Personal Opinion

The first danger would be to elevate my opinion above the overall teaching of the Scripture—to bring the Scriptures under the judgment of my personal opinion. Everyone has an opinion, and many of us would rather die than give up our opinion. Now, where do we get these opinions of ours? Perhaps some pastor under whom we were saved and grew to know the Lord through his ministry instilled within us his opinion on certain subjects. That pastor's opinion, as far as we are concerned, trumps the Word of God itself. This is a grave danger.

Actually, nobody has an opinion of his or her own. Every opinion we have has come from somewhere else or someone else. Through the years, I have had to die to many opinions that really were not rooted in the plain teaching of the Bible. When first saved, we are so eager to accept the doctrinal teachings of the church we are attending that we never stop to think through or pray through some of these issues.

It is wonderful to have opinions on politics and sports and literature and music. All of these opinions are based upon personal preference, likes and dislikes. Somebody will be a sports fan of a certain football team simply because his father was a fan of that team. Now, that team may not have won a game in 13 years, but the person is still a fan of that team; and in his opinion, it is the best team in any field. It is an opinion imposed upon them from some outward force.

Be careful of your opinions.

## It Leads to a Rift in Christian Fellowship

Another danger associated with this is that many times it separates Christians from other Christian fellowship. For example, if you are a Calvinist, you are warned to stay away from all Arminians, and vice versa. I often hear, "I'm a Calvinist because it's the only true way." And of course, if Calvinism is the only way, then Arminians must certainly be heretics of the first order.

We must remember that anything that divides our fellowship is our enemy. Anything that comes between Christian brothers has to be renounced for what it is and given over to the Lord. I'm not suggesting we should not have opinions about certain things; what I am saying is that if our opinions divide us from good Christian fellowship, something somewhere is wrong. Perhaps that opinion needs to be surrendered to the Lord.

I believe the worst danger of this is seen in our projection out into the world. Instead of preaching the simple gospel to reach a lost world, we are tempted to develop Calvinism or Arminianism. Then I say, of what value is that? The world certainly does not need Arminianism. And it surely does not need Calvinism. What the world needs is Jesus Christ. Then anything that divides our attention and energies from lifting up Christ in this world is something we need to deal with immediately.

## It Offends Our Father God

Perhaps another problem this brings to us would be that it offends the Father. What we are in fact doing is asking the Father to choose between two sons. This, of course, God will never do. Jesus Christ did not suffer on the cross so that we could fight over doctrinal positions. He did not rise from the dead so that we could usurp our doctrinal superiority over another brother.

In order to assure ourselves from falling into the rut of twisting and turning the Scriptures, we should be grounded in good, solid Bible teaching. But I am not for the kind of Bible teaching that excludes other fine Christians from our fellowship or that forces the Father to choose which son or daughter is the better son or daughter. Notice, the writer to the Hebrews says, "We are persuaded better things of you."

## God Our Deliverer
Charles Wesley (1707–1788)

Whither, oh, whither should I fly,
But to my loving Saviour's breast,
Secure within thine arms to lie,
And safe beneath thy wings to rest?

I have no skill the snare to shun,
But thou, O Christ, my wisdom art;
I ever into ruin run,
But thou art greater than my heart.

I have no might t'oppose the foe,
But everlasting strength is thine;
Show me the way that I should go,
Show me the path I should decline.

Foolish and impotent and blind,
Lead me a way I have not known;
Bring me where I my heaven may find,
The heaven of loving thee alone.

# 7

# FAITHFUL IN TRUTH AND LOVE

*For God is not unrighteous to forget your work and labour of love,*
*which ye have shewed toward his name, in that ye have ministered*
*to the saints, and do minister.*

HEBREWS 6:10

If I were writing to preachers, to young preachers particularly, I would say to them, "There are two things required of you before your congregation. One is to always speak the truth. The other is to always speak the truth in love." You have heard the truth spoken in a hostile manner where the one speaking gave the impression that he was very angry with the congregation; and if they were going to hell, it was all right with him. And if they were going to backslide, he would wash his hands of it.

This the man of God never does. He preaches the truth in love. No Christian is ever required of God to listen to a man who does not preach in love. Neither should there be preaching in love at the sacrifice of truth. Either way there comes a danger of going off into deep water.

The writer to the Hebrews was faithful both in truth and in love. He pointed to their failure to love and their impeded spiritual growth, and it was not easy for him to do it. He showed them the grave danger they had placed themselves in. Apostasy and shipwreck could lie ahead if they did not watch out, because it has done so for many. Then he set out to rescue them. You will hear or feel the eager yearnings of the man of God.

Yet, I do not give the credit only to the man who wrote the book of Hebrews, because I hear the beating pulse of something bigger and grander than the man himself. It is nothing else but the love and care and compassion of the holy God, who is looking down upon us with all the anguish of the Father over his lost sons, all the anxious care of the Shepherd over his lost sheep, and all the brooding love of the Spirit over the lost coin. One thing we may always be sure of, whether we listen to and heed the Word of God or not, God is always brooding over us with the anguished care of the triune God.

The writer becomes a physician to the souls of these men and women. He speaks to them with tender affection. He encourages them with thoughts of God's fairness to them. God is not unrighteous to forget their work and labor of love.

I remember once listening to a man preach. He was preaching for a week, and he spent the entire week proving that the audience did not have anything at all. We were spiritual paupers—hopeless, worthless—and nobody there was a spiritual person. From the pastor to the janitor, we were all a bunch of backslidden, carnal, worldly, deceptive, double-dealing people. I sat there and finally closed up on the brother. He had not been there long enough to know us that well. Even if we were that bad, he had no way of finding out. A medical physician does not do that. He never tells a man he is sicker than he is. He deals with the man where he finds him, as near as he can.

This man of God in Hebrews spoke to these people with tender affection. You will find it written here, "but ye, beloved." He encouraged them that God had not forgotten them, and He would remember what they had done. Maybe they were not praying as much as they should, but they were praying more than they used to. Maybe they were not giving as much as they could, but they were giving more than they had before. Maybe they were not all they should have been, but they were not what they had been before they were converted. Maybe they had slipped back a little in their way, but they were not way back yonder in Adam's graveyard. God had brought them out and made something out of them. This is what the man who wrote the book of Hebrews says to them as their physician.

There is a beautiful word found among our Anglican friends. It is the word "curate." I was fascinated with the origin of the word. "A curer, somebody that goes about and cures people." He is a physician of souls of the gospel he preaches, and through prayer and through love, he cures people; he cares for them as a physician cares. This is always the work of God. If the Lord smites you, it is so He can cure you. If the Lord rebukes you, He does it that He may teach you. If He disciplines you, He does it so that you may be made holy and made partakers of His holiness. The writer says in this text, "And we desire that every one of you do shew the same diligence to the full assurance of hope unto the end" (Heb. 6:11).

## Three Levels of Spiritual Food

There are likely to be three classes of people among religious people. Ideally, everybody ought to be in the first class, but that is not usually the case. These few will find the excellent riches of the heavenly gifts. They find it by the Word of God and prayer, by surrendering, and by faith going on in the things of God. However, there is a larger number who are satisfied with mere crumbs.

I once read a story that D. L. Moody told about a dog. Every day this man fed his dog the crumbs and scraps from the table. Nothing but crumbs and scraps from off the table. The dog would sit patiently, sad-eyed, when the meal was over. They would pile the scraps up and he would go out into the kitchen and have his meal. One day, they had company and were talking about the dog eating the scraps. One suggested as a trial that they offer him a steak. So they prepared for him a plate with a nice, well done, sizzling steak on it.

The visitor said, "I will bet you, the dog will not eat it."

"Oh," the owner said, "surely he will. He will be so glad to get it after the scraps."

They set the plate down containing the sizzling steak, and the dog looked at it and then looked up questioningly into the eyes of his master and then turned around and sat down a little way off. He had lived on scraps until he could not even believe there was such a thing as a steak.

I believe this is possible; we can be satisfied with spiritual scraps. God will feed us according to the way we take it. If we have been used to scraps and we have lived on scraps and have developed an appetite for scraps, then that is exactly what we get.

That is the second class, and they are the Lord's people, all right, but they have not found and are not particularly looking for the excellent riches of the heavenly gifts.

But I notice a third class, large in number in many churches. They have only vague information of divine truth, only shadows instead of realities, only groundless hopes instead of guaranteed possessions. The apostle desires here that every one of them should come into the first class. He is not satisfied that they should classify themselves as "very good Christians" and "not so good Christians" and "poor Christians." He wants everyone to be first-class Christians looking for the excellent riches of the heavenly gifts.

## Live Like Those Who Inherit the Promises

Let us suppose that in the church you attend, only 1 out of 100 should fail. The other 99 should make it through into the excellencies of the riches of Christ. That would be a most marvelous thing, and it would be a statistical triumph to find that 99 percent of the membership of that church were blessed, Spirit-filled Christians. Only 1 out of 100 was failing. But for the one that failed, it would be a personal tragedy.

It is possible to have an airplane crash and all survive but one. And if there are 70 on board, the newspapers happily report, "only one was killed." But if that one was your husband, it would not be a statistical triumph; it would be a personal tragedy.

If the boat sank with 12 people on it, and all escaped safely to shore but one, that would be a statistical triumph. But if that one were your teenage boy on a fishing trip, and they had to drag the lake to find him, and after several days they had pulled him up, that would be a personal tragedy.

So, it is entirely possible for us to have a high percentage of spiritual people in the church. But if there is even one that is not, that is a personal tragedy for that one. And if you should be that one, I say that you would be visited with a tragedy greater than was ever conceived by the mind of Shakespeare.

The Scriptures admonish us to see these treasures: "And we desire that every one of you do shew the same diligence to the full assurance of hope unto the end: that ye be not slothful, but followers of them who through faith and patience inherit the promises" (Heb. 6:12). Not sloth, but diligence, and followers of the best Christians, the best people.

When I think of treasure hunters, I suppose that never a year goes by but the media comes out with some new treasure being hunted. Some vessel reported to have sunk off a certain shore. They go out with radar and electronic equipment to try to locate it. Then deep-sea divers go down, hoping to discover something. Explorers have left their homes, suffered, labored and even died in order to find treasure. And the adventurers have dived to the floor of the ocean, and prospectors have searched in the earth for a lifetime.

If you go to the southwest of the United States, you will find the old "Desert Rats" as they call them. They have lived in the desert and panned for gold all their life. It is in their blood, and they cannot escape it. They are after gold. Maybe they find enough to keep their soul and body together, and the skin to cover it, but not enough to get a shave or a haircut or decent clothing or decent anything. They search for a lifetime for gold they never find in quantities to do them any good.

I suppose if there is any humor in hell, I can imagine there would be roars of demonic laughter to see how human beings, made in the image of God, dig for a lifetime for gold and then melt it into gold bars and hide it back in the earth from which they spent a lifetime looking for it. It seems to me that for men made in the image of God, and made to seek the high heaven above as their home, this is one of the supreme tragedies of the world. We dig it out of the ground at great loss and sacrifice and then bury it back in the ground again. What good is it, lying down there? You cannot eat it. You cannot wear it. You cannot inject it into a dying man to bring him back to health. You cannot pull it over his cold baby at night. There it is. Sacks of gold to be hidden; riches that could never bring peace, never bring rest, safety, life or happiness.

Men have forsaken all and searched with great diligence for these things. But the Holy Spirit says, "We desire that every one of you do shew the same diligence to the full assurance of hope unto the end, that ye be not slothful, but followers of them who through faith and patience inherit the promises" (Heb. 6:11-12).

## Where True Riches Reside

What do we look for? I read in the book of Ephesians, "Blessed be the God and Father of our Lord Jesus Christ, who hath blessed us with all spiritual blessings in heavenly places in Christ" (Eph. 1:3). I also read, "That the God of our Lord Jesus Christ, the Father of glory, may give unto you the spirit of wisdom and revelation in the knowledge of him: The eyes of your understanding being enlightened; that ye may know what is the hope of his calling, and what the riches of the glory of his inheritance in the saints, and what is the exceeding greatness of his power to us-ward who believe, according to the working of his mighty power" (Eph. 1:17-19).

These are the things that matter. Though you are as poor as the proverbial church mouse, and though you die in a concentration camp or a prison, and though your poor body is dragged out and thrown over a cliff for the buzzards to pick on, you are still richer than any riches found by explorers and adventurers or prospectors or financial geniuses could make you. What treasure do we look for? Of what am I speaking? The riches of pardon, inward freedom, endless life in a glorious home and immortality at last. And we even know where it is. We do not have to go prospecting for it.

I have never liked the word "adventure" when used of religion. Sometimes men get poetic and talk about the "adventure of knowing God." No, an adventure means I go out not being sure of what I am after or what I will find or whether I will find it or where I will find it, and there will possibly be great danger to me. Maybe I will not find anything, and maybe I will die in the attempt. Maybe the buzzards will pick my bones in the desert and all that will be left of me are the buttons off my clothes and a bit of leather the buzzards could not eat. Or maybe I will get some treasure, but on my way in I will be overtaken by bandits, and they will kill me and take my treasure and leave my bones there. That is what "adventure" means. It means going out, looking for trouble—joyful, thrilling trouble—with maybe a bit of reward attached.

Do not think of religion as an adventure. There is no element of uncertainty in following Christ. He is the Victor. He has won. And the battle is His, with no possibility of loss or failure. I know where to go. I do not go out looking with the divining rod as the farmer does for water. I do not go out with a Geiger counter as the man looking for metal. No, I know where to go. I do not have to look for it. I know where it is. I know that Jesus Christ is made unto me wisdom, righteousness, sanctification and redemption. I know that God has put into His Son, Jesus Christ, all I need for now and forever.

We know that He is the eternal God made flesh and dwelt among us. We know that time and space, love and life, hope and peace, riches and bliss and all that the human soul could need or crave is found in the person of Jesus Christ. Our mistake is that because it is there, we think we have it, when the fact is, we may not have it at all. It may be in Christ, but not in us. The Holy Spirit through the man of God urges us that we be not slothful, but diligent and press on to the full assurance of hope unto the end, through faith and patience we might inherit the promises.

Now the Holy Spirit says, "Put away sloth." I do not know if the half-dead animal that spends its lifetime in the state of a coma, hanging upside down by its heels, was named after the word "slothful," or if somebody looked at it and named it "sloth" because of the word "slothful." But if you want to know what slothfulness means, look at that poor creature that hardly knows what it is, hanging upside down practically all the time.

The warning is, "Do not be a sloth." Do not hang there in a state of semi-activity, but be diligent, earnest, eager and careful.

I knew of a family in the city of Chicago, Illinois. They were a tragically poor and pitiful household, but something in them burned like a light. They were Christians, and the two boys wanted an education. They had no money. The old, weary, deaf father had to do odd jobs for a living. But those boys started in. One used to leave one class and run 10 minutes to get to the next class without anything to eat, and go through days with nothing but a hot dog if he could afford that, from early breakfast to late supper. They dressed in the most ordinary clothes.

Both boys pressed through. They studied late at night. They studied early in the morning. They withdrew themselves from ordinary social contact. They were going to have an education regardless of the cost. The result was that one became principal of a high school and the other worked with highly classified scientific information for the government during the war and became a professor at the University of Ohio. They got their education, but they did not loaf; they were diligent. If young people would give half as much persistence and continued activity in knowing God as these brothers did to getting an education, they would be among the leaders of their generation for God.

Writers go through tremendous effort and discipline to get down in print what they want to say. The long vigil, the exhausting corrections, the times of getting up from a typewriter and walking around in circles, wondering where the sequence of the sentence ever disappeared to. If writers are going to write anything that anybody will read, they are going to have to give birth to it. And so it is with any profession. If you are going to make good, you will have to pour everything into it.

Yet some will claim, "We despise the world, we have eternal life, we are forgiven and heaven is our home; we are going to wear a crown some bright morning." But where is the diligence? The scientists of the world put them to shame. The students pursuing an education put them to shame. The writer puts them to shame. Even the ballplayer out in the ballpark puts them to shame.

Let's say I asked a young man, "Listen, son. I want you to serve God now."

"All right," he says. "I would like to be a Christian. What am I to do now? Get baptized and go to church?"

"Yes, all that. Then I want you to put as much into serving God as a quarterback puts into his football game. And if you get knocked down, smile, get up and keep going."

But when a young man wants to become a Christian, we say to him, "Put away smoking and drinking and all that like kind of stuff, and live a disciplined life." And he whimpers like a baby and says, "What you want is too hard." We're told we will drive everybody away if we preach like that.

Boxers do not smoke or drink or run around nights or lie around in nightclubs. They work diligently. What for? For the glory of getting in there and having a 50/50 chance of knocking the other man unconscious, or getting knocked unconscious while a few onlookers clap their cigarette-stained hands and shout. But when we ask Christians to put anything into their Christianity, they begin to run like hens thrown off their nest, clucking in every direction, making the feathers fly, and saying, "Oh, you will drive the young people away." I do not believe it. Young people, if they are worth their salt, and worth saving, are ready to put something into their Christianity.

So be diligent and press on to the full assurance of your hope in Christ. The result of this diligence is a faith that is strong and willing to inherit the fulfillment of the promises.

### Stand Up, My Soul, Shake Off Thy Fears
Isaac Watts (1674–1748)

Stand up, my soul, shake off thy fears,
And gird the gospel-armour on,
March to the gates of endless joy
Where thy great Captain-Saviour's gone.

Hell and thy sins resist thy course,
But hell and sin are vanquish'd foes,
Thy Jesus nail'd them to the cross,
And sung the triumph when he rose.

What tho' the prince of darkness rage,
And waste the fury of his spite,
Eternal chains confine him down
To fiery deeps, and endless night.

What tho' thine inward lusts rebel,
'Tis but a struggling gasp for life
The weapons of victorious grace
Shall slay thy sins, and end the strife.

Then let my soul march boldly on,
Press forward to the heavenly gate,
There peace and joy eternal reign,
And glittering robes for conquerors wait.

There shall I wear a starry crown,
And triumph in almighty grace,
While all the armies of the skies
Join in my glorious leader's praise.

# 8

# FAITH IS A JOURNEY FOR THE HEART

*Through faith we understand that the worlds were
framed by the word of God, so that things which are seen
were not made of things which do appear.*

HEBREWS 11:3

Nowhere in Scripture is there any kind of a definition of "faith." It simply states that faith is the substance of things hoped for and the evidence of things not seen (see Heb. 11:1). It does not give us the definition of faith, just as the words "God is love" do not give us the definition of "God" or of "love." The Bible has very few definitions. Definitions have to do with philosophy and reason, whereas the Bible is a spiritual book directed to the heart.

Certainly the Bible contains morals and ethics. "Ethics" is another word for "righteousness," and "morals" concerns "good and bad." The Bible is not a book of reason about good or bad. The Bible is an authoritative book telling us what is good and what is bad. We need no textbook on ethics when we come to the Word of God. God has written the only textbook there is that is valid and binding upon all men.

Faith is demonstrated, not defined, and I should like to point out that this is God's ideal for His Church. Faith or love should not be defined from the pulpit, but practiced by the people in the pew as well as by the man in the pulpit. So we have here faith, the substance of things hoped for.

The newly enlisted Marine proposes to a young woman before he leaves for duty and seals that proposal with an engagement ring. That ring is a promise of an event to come. The young woman wears this ring with a great deal of pride, showing it to everybody. The date has been set for the wedding, and the whole thing is in motion.

What if someone came to this newly engaged woman and said, "I really don't believe you're going to get married. I think it's all a hoax. Your boyfriend has no intention of marrying you. He's not even here."

I'm sure the young woman, newly engaged, would not be daunted by this kind of talk. After all, she has the ring, the promise. She could turn to this kind of talk and simply say, "Here's my engagement ring. This ring says that I'm going to get married."

All of her hopes rest in that engagement ring. Every time she looks at that ring it reminds her of a special event to come.

"But," someone could object, "you're not married now."

"Ah, but I'm going to be on such and such a date."

That engagement ring reminds her of the promise from her husband-to-be. That ring is the tangible expression of her wedding day. Certainly, the ring does not take the place of that wedding day, but it points to that time with a great deal of promise and assurance. It is the evidence of something wonderful to come for her in the days ahead. It brings into her life the supreme confidence that she is soon to be married.

That example does not define faith and does not even describe it. It simply tells how faith is demonstrated. It is by faith that we have to walk here on earth.

## Ignorance by God's Design

I like to think that God compels us to live in a wonderful state of benign ignorance. Some do not like to hear this, but it is true. When it comes to ignorance, there is a wide variety.

There is the ignorance of the man who refuses to learn because it would upset his prejudice. Then there is the ignorance of the person who has never been anywhere much; he lives or stays in the country and the woods. He is intelligent, but he is ignorant. There is a difference between ignorance and a lack of intelligence. "Ignorance" means "not knowing."

For instance, I am quite ignorant on space flight. All I know is what I read in the papers and hear over the radio; I could not run one of those flights. I would overshoot the moon 20,000 miles and come down in some mountain if I were running it. But I do not sit by with my chin down on my chest saying I am unintelligent. It is not unintelligence, just lack of training.

God keeps us in a state of benign ignorance. By that I mean, we are ignorant of everything that matters, but we know the things that do not matter. That is the odd thing. The things that matter we do not know and cannot know so "that no flesh should glory in his presence . . . [but] he that glorieth, let him glory in the Lord." There has always been conflict between human reason and God. Human reason has always been the rival of God, trying to take God's place. Adam's race fell the day the devil persuaded Adam and Eve that if they would eat of the fruit of the Garden they would become as gods, knowing all things. They fell for Satan's lie and took the bait. Instead of being as gods, knowing all things, they fell down to the level where they could not know anything that really mattered at all.

Consequently, man's pride has hindered him from coming to know God in any sense of intimacy. God has not allowed him to understand one fundamental fact of life. What is life? I do not know; nobody knows. You cannot explain life, because you cannot understand life. You can explain anything you understand. You can define anything you can understand. But life is one of those glorious things that escape our understanding.

You know you have consciousness, but you do not know what consciousness is. Consciousness is awareness, but what is awareness? Awareness is consciousness, and so we define one with the other and arrive back where we started.

I am not trying to be facetious; it is literally true.

Then there is love. Nobody knows what love is, and nobody knows if it is a thing or not. When we try to explain it or define it, we look foolish; yet it is wonderful that we can enjoy and experience things we cannot define. To experience without understanding is the act of a child. The child eats its food and has not the remotest idea what is in it or whether it is good for him or not. He experiences many of life's varied facets and does not understand any of them. He just enjoys.

My father used to say about horses, when he saw them pulling and leaning forward in their great body, if a horse only knew his own strength he could not handle it. So God smiles at our feeble reasoning that compels us to live like children. And that is as God would have it. Jesus said, "Except ye be converted, and become as little children, ye shall not enter into the kingdom of heaven" (Matt. 18:3).

While the learned college professor tries to come in head-first and never gets in at all, the simple-hearted man who is willing to experience and let God understand can spend a happy lifetime in the church of Christ, and a happy eternity at the throne of God.

## The World's Sub-Faith

Those who boldly reject faith in all of its ramifications, criticizing and making fun of those who insist on living by faith, actually are compelled to live by what I call a "sub-faith." There are pseudo-thinkers today who scorn religion because they say it requires faith, and they do not believe in faith. Yet, they are compelled every day to live by faith. They expect the sun to be in a certain position each morning when they get up. They do not give much thought to the food they eat, but they expect it to be there. Every day they have a certain expectation concerning every aspect of their life. This expectation is a sub-faith, and God hates it.

This sub-faith is not a high-level faith; it is not saving faith. But it is a kind of faith.

The man walks on the sidewalk, expecting that sidewalk to hold him up. He never gives any thought to it because he does not believe in faith. He believes in reason.

He argues that religion is passé, an old burned-out thing, because it does not rest on reason as he does. Reason is his God. Actually, he only goes by reason from the time he gets up in the morning and shakes himself awake. Up until then, he has been living by faith, a kind of sub-faith, and certainly not saving faith. We must distinguish biblical faith from every other kind of faith.

Those who worship reason as their God find themselves in terrible bondage. Some things cannot be understood by reason. That is where faith takes charge.

## Reason Is the Servant of Biblical Faith

When we come to the kingdom of God, the god "reason" takes the role of a servant. Reason does serve a purpose even in the kingdom of God, but it must be our servant, never our master. Christianity is not unreasonable, but neither is our life built upon that which we can reason out. Rather, the Christian plunges into a realm where reason is a servant. The Christian lives by his faith and not by reason. At the border of reason, faith takes charge. For the believer, faith has become an organ of knowledge opening up vast areas of understanding unattainable by reason itself.

What I cannot know by reason, I can know by simply believing. The writer to the Hebrews says that "through faith we understand" (Heb. 11:3). This is the great mystery of the Christian's walk of faith. Christian faith becomes an organ of knowledge. By faith, we understand all things that God has set before us. Let me be clear that faith is not a substitute for reality. There will come a time when faith gives way to sight.

Hebrews 11:3 tells us that through faith "we understand that the worlds were framed by the word of God, so that things which are seen were not made of things which do appear." Obviously, the writer had in mind here the world's doctrine of the eternity of matter. If you will remember, there was a doctrine held that matter is eternal, that there never was a time when things were not.

We all were, and all that we see is the result of a rearrangement of matter that never began to be, but always was. There is no invisible, eternal world behind the visible temporal world. But the Holy Spirit here in these verses from Hebrews gives us the truth that the visible came out of the invisible. The things that are seen came out of the things that were not seen. Matter came out of spiritual, and before all things, God was.

Faith certainly does not create these things and does not imagine these things. This is not a matter of imagination. The recently engaged woman is not imagining that she will one day get married. The engagement ring she wears is evidence of that which will be. She cannot create something just by believing it strongly enough. "Just put your mind to it," people are encouraging us today. "All you need to do is project yourself out of your subconscious and it will happen."

I once took in a series of lectures on the subconscious. The lecturer said the subconscious was that consciousness that lies underneath your consciousness and is the boss of your whole life. Oddly enough, your subconscious sits around listening for your consciousness to talk to it. If your consciousness says to your subconscious, "You are going to feel good today; you will feel good all day," then you will feel good today.

That was the philosophy of Émile Coué de Châtaigneraie (1857–1926), a French psychologist and pharmacist who introduced a method of psychotherapy and self-improvement based on optimistic autosuggestion.

His motto was, "Every day and in every way, I am getting better and better." He even had a rosary made out of string. He said, take a string and tie knots in it; and when you get up in the morning, take hold of your string and go down, feeling the knots. Every time you come to a knot, say, "Every day and in every way, I am getting better and better."

It is an odd thing, but he just dropped off one day and ceased to be around. Instead of, "Every day and in every way, I am getting better and better," he got deader and deader and was not now as good as he was before, at least physically. That is the way they apply it. The subconscious is waiting around for your consciousness to talk to it. When you eat, talk to your stomach and say to it, "Now, stomach, digest this; blood run and acids flow." He advised that if we talk to our stomach, our subconscious will carry it along. I have never talked to my stomach in my life, and I have always managed to digest my food all right unless, of course, I overate and did not deserve to digest it.

I know a better way. Keep your eyes on better things and just ignore yourself. You can get so body-conscious and so self-conscious that you get bogged down to your neck in quicksand. Instead of telling your stomach, "Digest, eat," thank God and go about your business and He will take care of the rest. Humanity has been doing it now since Adam and Eve walked the earth, and it will continue to do it for a long time to come, if the Lord tarries.

## Eyes to See What Is Really There

Faith is not an organ of imagination, but rather an organ of knowledge. It enables us to see with the eye of faith what is really there. This faith does not project imaginary things, look at them and then say, "There they are." There are no illusionary tricks to produce something that does not exist. Through the eye of faith, we can see the reality of things.

The millenniums to come are not a projection out of ourselves through our imagination, but we do see the millennium to come by the eye of faith and know it will surely come. Nobody projects out of himself the idea of heaven and then says, "Some day I'm going to go to heaven." I surely would not want to go to a heaven that had been projected out of my finite imagination. I am looking for something more substantial. Jesus said, "If I go and prepare a place for you, I will come again, and receive you unto myself; that where I am, there ye may be also" (John 14:3). After He said that, He went and did just that. How do I know He did all of this? It is by faith. Faith is the instrument that allows me to know this is true. I know because He said it was so, and He has never failed on anything yet.

Everything that is now promised through the Word of God, the hands of our Lord has fulfilled or will fulfill in the future. Faith is simply counting on His trustworthiness—believing that what He said is what He has already done for us.

We are not living in the world of imagination; it is the world that lives in imagination. I hear and read things that I do not believe; I have not any faith in it. I heard a speech made by Dag Hammarskjold, acting secretary of the United Nations, on the radio. It was a good speech all right; he said some nice things you would expect him to say. But it was all imaginary. We take for granted things that are not so and build on them. We take for granted that all people mean well, and if we just trust people we will be all right.

There are people who do not mean well. Only a fool would take it for granted that Khrushchev meant well, or Stalin meant well, or Hitler meant well, or any of them meant well. They meant to conquer and enslave people. Only an idiot with a man rushing at him with a bloody knife would stand and say, "He means well." It will be the last thing he ever says. Some people do not mean well. Evil men and seducers shall wax worse and worse until the end comes.

Read the book of Revelation and see if all men mean well. All you have to do is stroke their dander a bit, scratch their necks, and they will be all right. No, my brother, you must face reality. There is a reality that we can see and grasp; then there is the reality that we cannot see or grasp but we can believe. I want to live for that reality; for all things, however real, however many Hitlers and Stalins and Lenins and the rest, are only temporary. They were real, but they were temporary, and they are gone now. But that eternal city that hath a foundation whose builder and maker is God did not begin on the earth and will not end on the earth. It is not a victim of time nor a child of the passing years. It came out of the heart of God, and the mansions there were made by the hands of God for the people of God. By faith, we know this.

Faith is an organ of knowledge; so we are not imaginary or filled with vain imaginings, running about trusting things that are not so, pulling ourselves up by our own shoelaces. We are those who have heard the voice from beyond matter. The voice from beyond creation. The voice that called creation into being. We have heard that voice and we believe that voice that says matter was not eternal. There is only one eternal, and that is God. Matter is the handiwork of the eternal. And the things visible were made by the things invisible. Things that are spiritual made the things that are material. So Christians live for another world than this. When we hear God's voice speaking tenderly to our hearts, we are hearing the same voice that powerfully called creation into being.

I see another city. Abraham saw it and never would live in a city after that. He lived in tents from that hour on. Maybe someone might have said, "Abraham, why don't you build a city?" I can hear him saying, "After seeing that city not made with hands, I would be ashamed to dwell in another city. I will stick by my tent, just an old tent, until I see that city that has foundations whose builder and maker is God."

That is faith. We are saved by faith, and the Lord says to me, "Believe on me, follow me." Faith is not a journey for the feet, but a journey for the heart. Faith is not an act of reason, but an act of the will; and following is not an act once done, but a continuous act that begins when we are converted. It never ends while the long ages roll.

Faith is the substance; faith is the assurance; faith is the rock foundation; faith is that which translates the invisible into the visible, which takes things that are not and makes them as though they were. Faith translates the invisible world into the visible; and so by the eye of faith, I can see what God has wrought.

### Jerusalem the Golden
Bernard of Cluny (12th century)

Jerusalem the golden, with milk and honey blest,
Beneath thy contemplation sink heart and voice oppressed.
I know not, O I know not, what joys await us there,
What radiancy of glory, what bliss beyond compare.

They stand, those halls of Zion, all jubilant with song,
And bright with many an angel, and all the martyr throng;
The Prince is ever in them, the daylight is serene.
The pastures of the blessed are decked in glorious sheen.

O sweet and blessed country, the home of God's elect!
O sweet and blessed country, that eager hearts expect!
Jesus, in mercy bring us to that dear land of rest,
Who art, with God the Father, and Spirit, ever blessed.

# 9

# THE UNSETTLING NATURE OF FAITH

*By faith he forsook Egypt, not fearing the wrath of the king:*
*for he endured, as seeing him who is invisible.*

HEBREWS 11:27

Real faith not only does something for us, but it also does something to us. Faith is not passive. As the old Lutherans said, "Faith is a perturbing thing." You are perturbed until your faith finds its object in Jesus Christ and then comes to peace. But it is first greatly disturbing, though it is also a glorious and saving thing.

Moses was an Israelite of the covenant son of Abraham. Indeed, that was his condition at the time the story opens. He was out of the land of promise. God had given to Abraham what we now call the Holy Land, and Moses was supposed to be in the Holy Land where God had told Abraham, his father, that he would have him. But Moses was out of that land, down in Egypt, and disassociated from his people. He was in the court of Pharaoh, and his people were scattered throughout the land of Goshen. He was cut off from the life of the blessed covenant. He was living among the heathen, surrounded by false gods.

I do not know where Moses got his awakening, but Hebrews 11:24 says, "Moses, when he was come to years." The day

Moses came of age, mentally or spiritually, he became strangely troubled. He had, as they say, a good thing going. He was the supposed son of Pharaoh's daughter and enjoyed all the luxuries of the court. I suppose he was dandled on the knee of many a king and potentate as he grew up. He had all that royalty could afford there in Egypt, one of the greatest if not the greatest country in the world at that time, and he could have taken things for granted. He could have grown old and fat and finally died in Egypt, still the son of Pharaoh's daughter. But when he came of age, he became spiritually awake.

We are not told how it happened, but it started almost unperceived by him and then grew and deepened until finally he kept saying to himself, "What am I doing luxuriating in the court of the heathen emperor when I belong with my own people because I am a Jew?" I do not know who told him he was a Jew. Maybe his real mother slipped the word to him when he was old enough to understand. There would not seem to be any reason for guessing about it, but he awoke to the fact that he was not where he belonged.

## A Great Spiritual Awakening

It was a great awakening for the man Moses, a vague but real hunger came to the man. It is a great hour for any man when he has a spiritual awakening.

Consider the vast multitudes of people. They come and go and build and plant and reap and sow and marry and give in marriage and travel and work and sleep and play and eat and laugh and do all the things that human beings do, but they never have any awakening at all by any inward voice. They are simply as

God made them, descended from Adam, and with a little education rubbed on for veneer, but no spiritual awakening.

Moses had such a spiritual awakening. He came to the knowledge of who he was. Before that, he just went along with things, accepting everything that was as it should be. It was perfectly all right, so he went along with it. Suddenly, it came to him what he could be and was not, and what he was that he should not be. That is a holy day in any man's life: to see through the pretenses of the world.

The world out there is running a confidence game, fleecing and staining and cheating and damning, and most people never see it at all. They are taken in just as innocently as a lamb led to the slaughter. And some few people, by the grace of God, awaken when they come of age and get sick of their own sins. Many people are saved on such a moral rebound.

Take anybody who knows he has sinned and who is sick with his sin. Upon conversion, his rebound is likely to take him way out beyond the border. That is exactly what happened to Moses. He said, "Here I am, living off the fat of the greatest land in the world, on false pretenses, claiming to be an Egyptian when actually I am a Jew trying to act like the son of the queen. I am no Prince; I am just a Jew from the loins of Abraham, and everything is wrong and mixed up." He came of age, thank God.

I suppose he began to hate the world and hate Egypt and hate that royal court with its cheap humor and hollow pretense, its lying promises, and said to himself, *I believe there is more hope in God and in the God of my father Abraham than there is here in the court of Pharaoh.* He came to a day that he marked on the calendar and said, *Today I stop pretending. I am no longer going to pretend that I am something I am not. Today I say goodbye to the court of Pharaoh.*

Pharaoh's daughter was his supposed mother and would have been the only mother he had known. I am quite sure it was not easy for him to leave her. I am quite certain it was hard to leave his friends, for he had friends and owed old Pharaoh and his people a great deal. And it was rather hard to walk out on them; but there comes a time when you are either going to walk out on some people or you are going to perish. Moses was caught in the meshes of the world, and the only way he could get out was by determined rebellion.

The only people who get to heaven are conquered rebels—people who have rebelled against their sin. The rebellion is not against God. It had been against God, but now it is against the enemy—against the world, the flesh and the devil.

Personally, I do not like to see a person converted too easily. The man who can be converted too easily can be unconverted just as easily. But a tough customer who comes hard when he gets converted, that is a decision that is usually true for the rest of his life. Paul was tough; and when he was converted, he never even looked back once; he went straight forward.

And so, Pharaoh's supposed grandson Moses was suddenly converted, and said, *I will no longer be a slave to the devil; I will no longer be a victim of sin; I will no longer let the world victimize me; and I will no longer bow down to the world; so I will say goodbye to my mother.* If Pharaoh's daughter was still alive, as she probably was, he had to go and bid her goodbye. I am sure she did not understand, and I can picture a crying scene in which she said, "Haven't we done everything for you that possibly could be done? You have dressed in the finest of silks. What more could we have done for you?"

Moses would have to say, "Mother, I do not want you to think I am ungrateful, but I have other blood in my veins, and I am not an Egyptian. I claim my share of the Covenant with my father Abraham; and if I stay with you, I have to give up the Covenant; I will not give it up." I think he probably kissed and hugged his old mother goodbye and then walked out and never went back until God sent him back to deliver Israel years later.

When God sent him back, Moses knew all about what to do. He knew what door to enter, where to find the Pharaoh; he knew everything because he grew up there as a lad. God certainly picked the right man to send back and say to Pharaoh, "Let my people go." Nobody else could have done it as well as a boy brought up there. They recognized him as soon as they saw him coming, and said, "There's that boy; he is older now, but there he is." When he said goodbye to his mother, he chose to go; "chose" is one of the pivotal words in religious life. Not only did he renounce something, but he also chose something else.

## We Choose What We Esteem

When you leave the old life, there must be a renunciation, and that is always a negative thing. But remember, you are not saved by what you renounce; you are saved by what you embrace. Moses not only renounced his life in Egypt and all it meant. He chose Jehovah, looking forward, looking ahead, as Abraham had, to the day of Christ. He chose the Covenant; he chose redemption; he chose to go along with the people of the Covenant; he chose to pay whatever it cost him and suffer affliction

A Disruptive Faith

with the children of God rather than enjoy the pleasures of sin for a season.

We usually make out sin to be a great burden, but sin is often a pleasurable thing. That is why it can be so dangerous. Moses chose the pleasures of God's kingdom rather than the pleasures of sin. He chose the afflictions of the Kingdom over the pleasures of sin. He esteemed the riches of Christ, the reproaches of Christ, to be greater riches than the treasures of Egypt. God said to him, "Moses, if you stay in Egypt, you will be rich; you have treasure here; but if you will come with Me, you will have reproach. Which will it be? Reproach with Me or treasures with Pharaoh?"

Moses said, "O God, as the son of Abraham, I choose reproach with the people of God." Therefore, he united himself with the people of God, identified with them rather than continue with the pleasures of sin, forsaking Egypt and not fearing the wrath of Pharaoh. That little phrase thrown in there seems to indicate that when the king heard Moses was gone, he raised heaven and earth to find him. He was trying hard to get him back, but it did not work because this man was "esteeming." That is, he set certain values.

We must set certain values with certain things. We must say, "Is this worth the cross to me?"

When you go shopping for something, you say, "That was just a trifle and it does not really cost much." But if it is anything that costs a great amount of money, you do some esteeming, and you do not grab the first thing and run. You set values and say, "Can I afford this? Well, I think maybe I can afford this, but I cannot afford that." What you are doing is putting a value on things. Moses, the man of God, had to do that.

118

"All right," God said, "you need to make up your mind. Are you going to loaf around, play and be at your ease, with everybody bowing to you? Or are you going to join my people, my minority group, where you will be reproached for your faith?" I do not think Moses made up his mind in five minutes. I think he might have said, "God, give me a day to think it over, maybe a week to think it over." I think it grew in him as he thought about it.

His values changed and he left the place of pleasure for the place of reproach. A wonderful paradox, he finds the reproach more pleasurable than the pleasures he enjoyed before. This is always the way with Christians.

I think there are hundreds of thousands of people everywhere who will not become Christians because they fear the reproach. The Bible does not have anything sympathetic to say about them. In Revelation 21:8, it says, "The fearful, and unbelieving, and the abominable, and murderers, and whoremongers, and sorcerers, and idolaters, and all liars, shall have their part in the lake which burneth with fire and brimstone." The man or woman who is afraid to follow the Lord because he or she is afraid of reproach will suffer loss; God cannot possibly do anything for that person. However, the man or woman who will follow Christ regardless of the reproach will be saved.

## "He Forsook"

Then there are those wonderful words, "he forsook." There is no salvation without abandonment, although the abandonment is not the salvation. There is no salvation without renunciation, but the renunciation is not the salvation. Forsaking, abandoning and renunciation are necessary before we can turn to the Lord.

Nobody stays on a sinking ship when it is obvious that it is going down. In the Air Force when a plane goes down, the flyer does not ride it to his death. He is taught to jump out, pull the string on the parachute and come floating down so that he can go up another day and try it again. But the only way to be safe from a falling plane is to get the parachute open. The only way to be saved from a burning house is to get up and get out of it. So Moses foresaw, he endured to see Him who was invisible.

Christians are odd people. They see things that cannot be seen and hear things that cannot be heard, and talk to a person that is invisible. They suffer reproach. Go to church once a week and nobody thinks about it. You are a good citizen. But take yourself seriously and go to church whenever the doors are open, people will say you need to see a doctor.

We must endure to see Him who is invisible. There are times when even your friends around you cannot be trusted. Not that they are false, but you do not quite know who to believe.

However, do not start saying, "I don't see how sister so-and-so can do what she does and be a Christian. I don't see how brother so-and-so can act the way he does and be a Christian." We are not converted by looking to our brother or sister. We are converted in order that we may look unto Jesus, the author and finisher of our faith. He will never disappoint. There will never be a day when we will say, "I don't see how the Lord does this." We will always say, "True and righteous are thy judgments" (Rev. 16:7) and "the path of thy commandments . . . therein do I delight" (Ps. 119:35). So let us endure, seeing Him who is in-

visible, and like Moses, we will come out all right and the glory
of God will be our reward.

## Thy Way, Not Mine, O Lord
Horatius Bonar (1808–1889)

Thy way, not mine, O Lord,
However dark it be;
Lead me by Thine own hand,
Choose out the Path for me.

Smooth let it be, or rough,
It will be still the best;
Winding or straight it leads
Right onward to Thy rest.

I dare not choose my lot;
I would not if I might:
Choose Thou for me, my God,
So shall I walk aright.

Take Thou my cup, and it
With joy or sorrow fill,
As best to Thee may seem;
Choose Thou my good and ill.

Choose Thou for me my friends,
My sickness or my health.
Choose Thou my cares for me,
My poverty or wealth.

Not mine, not mine the choice,
In things both great and small;
Be Thou my guide, my strength,
My wisdom and my all.

# 10

# FAITH PRODUCES SPIRITUAL HEROES

*By faith Abraham . . . by faith Moses . . . by faith the
harlot Rahab. . . . And what shall I more say? For the time would
fail me to tell of Gedeon, and of Barak, and of Samson, and of
Jephthae; of David also, and Samuel, and of the prophets:
Who through faith subdued kingdoms, wrought
righteousness, obtained promises, stopped the mouths of lions.*

HEBREWS 11:17,23,31-33

Like a man who has found a great treasure and returns to it a
thousand times to examine it, to count it and feel it, so do we
with these words "by faith." This is the mighty and triumphant
sound of God's people. "By faith" they did this, showing that
faith is not an imaginary thing, but dynamic and powerful, accomplishing things indeed.

In looking at these people in the eleventh chapter of Hebrews, notice how they differ from each other.

One snare of the Christian life is thinking that everybody
ought to be exactly alike. A quick look at the Scriptures will
completely disavow this idea. God never intended for everyone
to be precisely alike. Simply go to nature and see the hand of
God there. No two snowflakes are exactly alike. Go to the trees

of the forest. God did not create one tree. Rather, God created a forest of trees as different as night and day. Even if you planted the same trees next to each other, you would find that as they grow, they grow quite differently.

God does not repeat Himself in nature, and neither does He repeat Himself among His people. All of them have different strengths and different weaknesses. The thing they have in common is not the exterior but rather that interior passion for God. Look at the great heroes of the faith and you will find this to be absolutely true.

## Abraham and Jacob

Take, for example, Abraham and his grandson Jacob. You could not think of two men more widely separated in temperament. Abraham was a fine, dignified old gentleman who never bowed to do anything that was not proper, and you would like him. But his grandson Jacob was quite another character altogether. He was the supplanter. He was always doing embarrassing things that were not nice at all. That is, until the Lord made him into Israel. He was anything but a savory character, and yet God puts Jacob alongside Abraham, because God was busy making saints out of both of them. They were not alike except in one thing: They believed in God and had faith.

## Joseph and Moses

Then there was Joseph and Moses. Joseph was one of the gentlest of all men. You could not find a more gentle man than Joseph. He did not get angry with his brothers when they came down into Egypt.

Moses was not like Joseph at all. Moses was a man of fiery temper. He flew into a rage and slew an Egyptian. Later on, he smote a rock and said, "Ye rebels." He was a man not as gentle as Joseph was, yet God came to Joseph and Moses and blessed them both.

## Sarah and Rahab

We come to Sarah and Rahab, who are both mentioned here in the eleventh chapter of Hebrews. Sarah was a good woman, a woman against whom there is not a blot, while Rahab was a harlot. Yet both had faith and were converted and regenerated. Both were blessed by God.

Therefore, we have God working through His Spirit to bless and honor the differences in man as well as the likenesses. God accepts different personalities and manifests Himself to them.

I, for one, am sure glad we are not all alike. In your house, for example, are all kinds of electrical appliances as well as lights. They are all different. The toaster is not like an electric lamp. They all have a different function and purpose in that house. But they all run on the same electricity. The same power that runs the coffee maker runs your electric stove.

Likewise, Christians come in all sizes, shapes and forms. They differ one from another in race, language, perspective, talent and age. Yet, it is the same Holy Spirit within that empowers them to live a life for Christ. You cannot explain a person by his exterior alone.

At times, a Christian becomes enamored with the highly gifted and spiritual brother in the Lord. We admire him and even write his life story; but there is no way we would want anybody or everybody else to be just like him.

If you look at it from a congregational standpoint, we would not want everybody in our church to be like some old saint we admire. Quite frankly, we would find them to be quite a bit hard to live with in the same setting.

A young man desiring to become a preacher will often look at someone like Billy Graham and desire to be just like him. God made one Billy Graham and only one. God made one Billy Sunday. God made one A. B. Simpson. God made one D. L. Moody. If the truth were known, that was enough.

When somebody tries to copy one of his spiritual heroes, all he manages to do is copy his eccentricities. Never does he manage to imitate the power or usefulness of the man of God.

Do not try to be like anybody else except in these areas: We are to have faith, we are to love God and we are to obey Him. Apart from these, we are to be absolutely different.

## God Does Nothing that He Will Not Do Again

God, being who He is, never finds Himself in a rut. God's agenda does not change from one generation to the next. Man, created in the image of God, usually finds himself in a rut doing the same thing over and over again long after it has lost its significance and purpose. God is never like that. Men get so easily bored and are always looking around for some new contraption to entertain a flagging imagination. But God is not like that. God delights to do that which He has done in the past. One thing I have often taken comfort in is, whatever God has done for any of His people He will do for any of His people.

Although my life is vastly different from that of others, it is the same God working in me and through me. I can take great comfort in the fact that the God who worked in and through the apostle Paul is the same God who is working in and through me today.

I have often become a little discouraged after reading a biography of some great saint of the past. The reason being, I am comparing myself with that person. It is possible to be greatly harmed by reading the biography of some great man or woman of God of the past if we are tempted to compare ourselves with them. The great harm lies in the fact that all of us are very different and susceptible to different trials and temptations. Consequently, one man's victory is his own victory.

## God Works Through Each of Us

There was an old camp meeting song I enjoyed singing: "Let not conscience make you linger nor of fitness fondly dream." The temptation is to feel inferior, both morally and spiritually, to some of the great old saints of the past. My recommendation is that you put these things away from you. Do not allow the enemy of your soul to rob you of that unique quality God has breathed into you. Study the great men and women of the Bible and then go down and study the men and women throughout Church history and you will find one delightful thought. Each one was morally different and yet faith was the controlling factor of their life.

If you read the biblical accounts of Abraham and Moses and Samson and Sarah and Rahab, you will discover the vast differences between all of these people. God did not work the same way in them, and He will not work the same way through each one of us today. God has different tasks for us to do in the

Kingdom. All of these things are done through one primary spiritual ingredient, and that is faith.

I have seen it happen so many times. When the pastor of a church for 25 or 30 years dies or retires, the church board looks around for a new pastor. They finally call a young man to lead the flock. Then trouble begins. Some of the older people in church unintentionally injure the young man from doing the work God has called him to do. Through the years, they had become accustomed to the gravelly voice of the old man of the pulpit. Everything about him was quite familiar to them, and they had grown to love the old man.

The new pastor is not like the old pastor at all. Yes, he preaches from the same Bible and preaches the same gospel, but in the minds of some of the older people, there is a hindrance. They have become accustomed to the outward performance of a pastor who probably baptized and married them. Some of their kinfolk he officiated at their funerals. What the congregation needs to learn, and learn quickly, is that God does not bless someone because he is old or because he is young. He blesses people for their faith. He blesses them not because their voice is pleasant or gravelly, but for their faith. Unintentionally, the congregation can get in the way of what God wants to do.

There are saints now as well as then, but usually the ones that are saints do not call themselves saints except theologically, and they do not know that they are a great blessing to people. We can be in our day what those old heroes were in their day; and keep in mind that at the time, they did not know they were heroes. For instance, a simple little thing you do may bless people that you never dream it would.

Years ago, I wrote something called "Prayer of a Minor Prophet." At the time, I did not think too much of it; it just was something between God and me. I have received many letters and talked with people at Bible conferences and camp meetings that have been blessed by it. I never dreamed it would have such an effect. This only shows that some small thing you do may have a way of blessing people that you have never met before. And probably long after I am dead, people will be reading that little prayer of mine. This only shows that we can be in our day what the great saints of yesterday were in their day. God wants us to be holy in our life and filled with the Spirit, but He does not expect us to replicate any of the saints in the past. We must have the same faith, the same obedience, the same love they had; but after that, we must walk our own path.

I have given this quite some thought, and my conclusion is that it is always better to be a living dog than a dead lion. The reason I say that is because the dead lion was ferocious in his day, but that day is gone. A. B. Simpson was a great lion of the faith in his day. He literally reached the world with the gospel of Jesus Christ. But A. B. Simpson is now dead. His work, although great in its day, is over. We now must shoulder the responsibility without being intimidated by the great men and women of the past. We have a record of their faith in God, but we have a different path to walk. God expects us to walk that path with the same faith, love and obedience that these great men and women of the past showed.

When the Lord comes, we will not all be rewarded alike. Some people will deserve more than others under God's grace, and they will get it. In the meantime, let us thank God that we can take encouragement from the heroes of faith; and if we never rise to their level, thank God at least we rose as high as we did. It may very well be that some day you will rise as high as some of the people here in the eleventh chapter of Hebrews. And if another eleventh chapter of Hebrews were written, there would be people in it you would scarcely believe are in it. People like Rahab, what was she doing there? She was a harlot, but she believed God and turned hard toward faith. There was Gideon and there was Barak. There was Samson, who was not as perfect as he might have been, but he believed God and had faith and obeyed. So you would find some people that you did not think might be listed because the heroes of faith are not all dead. If you will believe God in the midst of an ungodly world and walk with the Lord in this time, as they walked with the Lord in their time, you will deserve a place if the Lord writes His final eleventh chapter of Hebrews.

## God's Work Always Goes On

This passage in the Old Testament has always brought a great deal of comfort to my heart: "And it came to pass after the death of Abraham, that God blessed his son Isaac; and Isaac dwelt by the well Lahairoi" (Gen. 25:11). As great and wonderful as was Abraham, the father of the faithful, he died, but God did not die with him. We find that God is speaking even to this very day. Sometimes we mourn the death of some great hero of the faith as though Christianity had come to a halt. Yes, those men and women were greatly used by God, and some of them in unusual ways that could never be replicated. But God did not die with them.

I remember that when the evangelist Dr. Paul Rader (1879–1938) died, I thought for a moment that would be the end of evangelism in this country. But he has been dead for some years now, and God is still working, moving and changing lives. Great men come and go, but God always remains on the front line. We have a generation before us to mightily impact for God that Paul Rader can never touch today. He's gone. His voice is silent. But God's voice is still speaking and continues to speak throughout all time.

How do you know what high, happy secret God wants to whisper into your heart? How do you know what God wants to say? What high expectations is He entertaining for you?

There are few things I would recommend more than these three things to take us far in accomplishing in our generation what God wants to do through us. They are: put away sin; separate yourself from the world; and offer yourself to God in faith with no strings attached.

Study the lives of the great men and women of the Scriptures throughout Church history and you will find quite an assortment of people with all kinds of temperaments, all kinds of trials and tribulations. A spirit of rebellion in some, and yet the mighty work of God was done through them. You will not find one perfect person in the whole lot. Some came close, and yet each one had his or her own particular flaw. God does not work through those who are flawless, but rather in spite of their imperfections. The heart that God uses is the heart yielded to Him in faith and obedience.

The person who thinks he or she has what it takes rarely has what it takes. None of those old saints of the past ever did anything great for God in their own strength. Why, look at Samson. On the outside, he looked like an ordinary man. But when the Spirit of God came upon him, he did extraordinary exploits. He was far from being the perfect man. He was far from being a man we would want to emulate in our daily life. How God used him is the mystery of divine leadership. God will find the man or the woman who yields himself or herself so completely because the only thing that matters in his or her life is God.

Thank God for the heroes of faith, but just remember that they are dead; they left their testimony behind them for the next generation, and for the next and for the next. You are alive, your generation is everywhere about you. You must serve your generation by the will of God before you fall asleep. You cannot serve another generation; you can only serve yours. Serve your generation and then leave your reputation and your service in the kind hand of God. And when the right day comes, He may put your name with the heroes of faith and say, "By faith he . . ." and "By faith she . . ." Whether He does or not, at least you will have the delight of knowing you pleased Him, and have the joy of knowing that you have served your generation.

### 'Tis by the Faith of Joys to Come
Isaac Watts (1674–1748)

'Tis by the faith of joys to come
We walk through deserts dark as night;
Till we arrive at Heav'n our home,
Faith is our guide, and faith our light.

The want of sight she well supplies,
She makes the pearly gates appear;
Far into distant worlds she pries,
And brings eternal glories near.

Cheerful we tread the desert through,
While faith inspires a heav'nly ray;
Though lions roar, and tempests blow,
And rocks and dangers fill the way.

So Abra'm, by divine command,
Left his own house to walk with God;
His faith beheld the promised land,
And fired his zeal along the road.

# 11

# THE CHALLENGE TO OUR FAITH

*Wherefore seeing we also are compassed about with so great a cloud
of witnesses, let us lay aside every weight, and the sin which doth so
easily beset us, and let us run with patience the race that is set before us,
looking unto Jesus the author and finisher of our faith; who for the joy
that was set before him endured the cross, despising the shame,
and is set down at the right hand of the throne of God.*

HEBREWS 12:1-2

The Scriptures often use metaphor in describing the Christian
life. Here, the writer uses the metaphor of a runner running in
a race. We are running the race of life. This image comes from
the Greek runners in the games that are similar to our Olympic
Games today.

Using this metaphor, we can see some of the dangers associated with our life of faith. Every Christian, for example, faces
the danger of losing the race. A runner runs expecting to win
the race. But there can be things hindering that runner from
finishing the race. It is important for us as Christians to understand this and find out what we can do to keep from losing the
race and be prepared for all obstacles.

Athletes go into a great deal of training both before and after a race. For many it is a lifetime commitment. The training is to prepare them for everything they might encounter on that track. Once the race is over, they do not quit but rather plunge back into a regimen of training. Every runner knows that he is in competition and only one person can win the prize.

In the Christian life there is a little bit of a difference. The Christian is not in competition with other Christians. As runners, we are competing in the race of life, but not in such a way as to pit us against each other. Our enemy is not another Christian or group of Christians. Yet, I have been in some places where I thought the people did not understand this. Our enemy, what we run against, is the world, the flesh and the devil in their various manifestations.

The Holy Spirit is faithful in equipping us to run this race. He knows the obstacles we will face and fully prepares us for the race. We are in training to defeat all of the hindrances that would keep us from finishing the race.

In the Bible, the race of life is never considered from the viewpoint of its speed. No Christian is ever to go out and try to break a track record. The Word of God says we are to run it with patience. The young man who, with the crack of the gun, goes tearing along at top speed and outdistances the rest by several yards is very likely, before the race is over, to be several yards behind, because he gave everything he had to begin the race. The race of the Christian faith is not a 100-yard dash; it is not a sprint at all. It is a long cross-country run. Speed must come in there somewhere, finally, but it can only come by patient steadfastness.

We must lay aside every weight, and the weight focused on here is not a sin. This imagery comes from the runner in the ancient Greek games. The Greek runners ran light. In fact, they ran all but naked. Clothing that was proper to wear at other times could not be used on the track, because every tenth of an ounce of weight held them back that much. So everything on them that could catch the wind, even though it did not weigh a small fraction of an ounce, was removed. They streamlined before the word was invented. We are running the race of life and are to lay aside the things that would hold us back or slow us down, make us begin to drag our feet and lose the race.

There are hindrances in the Christian life that are also sins, but the writer does not mention sin here in the first sentence. He mentions hindrances, which are not intrinsically sins. The difference between a spiritual Christian and an average Christian is that a truly spiritual Christian knows that he has not only to be delivered from sin, but he is also to be delivered from anything that would prevent him from winning.

## Not Everyone Runs to Win

The Holy Spirit here addresses an elect number. He never addresses the superficial man. Today, above all times in the history of the world, is the time of superficial religion. Religion is worn as a garment, a very light garment. Or it is to be considered as a little stream that results from a sudden thunderstorm that flows along and makes a lot of racket and stirs up a lot of dust. But it is so thin and shallow, give it just a little while and the sun will dry it out. Some people's souls are just like that.

The Holy Spirit never talks to the shallow man. If you are shallow, you cannot hear the voice of the Lord. The Holy Spirit never talks to the self-defender, the person who believes he is right and will defend his right to be what he is. He never talks to the arguer, to the afflicted person or to the insincere. Sincerity is an absolute prerequisite to the Christian life. If I am not sincere, I am ruled out. God runs a line through my name because God cannot have anything to do with insincere persons.

## Those Who Run Without Hindrances

Who is God addressing here? He addresses the meek. What do we mean by the meek? Translators have an awful time with the word "meek," but it means a kind person, a humble person, a lowly person. A lowly person is someone who thinks very poorly of himself; a humble person is someone who thinks poorly of himself in relation to others; and a meek person is someone who thinks lowly of himself or poorly of himself in his relation to God. So meekness and humility and lowliness are not virtues that are much chosen these days. They are not cultivated, nor do we desire that kind of Christianity. But the Holy Spirit cannot talk to the man unless he is a lowly man—he thinks lightly of himself; unless he is a humble man—he thinks poorly of himself with respect to others and, of course, before God. The Holy Spirit addresses the poor in spirit, and the sincere and reverent person, and the enlightened.

One of the saddest things I know of is the recent development of the type of song that is religious but flippant. It talks about God in a plaintively sad way, but it can smile while it is doing it. The song "When the Saints Go Marching In" was born in a camp meeting a long time ago. It is a typical camp meeting song, not a high-class hymn. It is one of those dramatic little numbers dealing with the second coming of Christ, but they have taken it and jazzed it up until now you do not recognize anything religious in it. Men who do not believe in God, whose lives are questionable and, in some cases, definitely evil, sing, "When the Saints Go Marching In," and even dance to it.

This, to my mind, is a serious matter. It is an affront against God, because reverence, that is, the fear of God in the sense of respect in the presence of God, is fundamental to any kind of real Christianity. If I am not a reverent man and have not a sense of solid respect when I think of God, or when I am in the presence of God, God cannot speak to me at all. I only give that one song as an illustration, but there are hundreds of them. There are people who have dedicated themselves to singing this kind of thing in nightclubs and before crowds, and the applauding crowds go on drinking their cocktails and smoking their cigarettes while applauding this thing. It is using religion without any reverence, without any sincerity and without any sense of solemnity.

God says, "I know thy works, that thou art neither cold nor hot: I would thou wert cold or hot. So then because thou art lukewarm, and neither cold nor hot, I will spue thee out of my mouth" (Rev. 3:15-16). God does not need our patronage and He does not need us to smile and nod toward Him. He is the great God Almighty who sits in the circle of the earth and sees the inhabitants thereof as but grasshoppers. They will be when He moves forth and His Son rides down the skies in a white horse with a sword at His side and on His thigh is written the name "Faithful and True." In that hour, when He calls the nations to judgment and puts some on the right hand and some on the left, those who have taken Him so lightly and irreverently will then cry out for the rocks and the mountains that they might be safe from the wrath of the Lamb.

## Things that Catch the Wind and Slow You Down

As long as something is simply theoretical and stays out of people's hair and does not insist on getting personal, everybody likes it. But we must have more than Bible exposition. We must have application. Therefore, I want to apply this metaphor that we must run the race free from all hindrances.

Let me give you some of those things that will encumber you in your walk of faith.

### Entertainment

One of the great traps of this generation can be summed up in one word: entertainment. A time was when most evangelical fundamentalists believed entertainment was a part of the world and not for the Christian—when you became a Christian, you gave up all worldly entertainment. They even preached against entertainment as something that would entrap the soul and rob you of the fullness of Christian joy. This now has undergone a very slow change. Little by little, worldly amusements have trickled into the church itself. Now there is hardly anything out in the world that Christianity is against. In fact, there is very little difference between many churches today and the world.

All of our efforts to become relevant to the world around us have had the effect of making us irrelevant in today's world. The premise has been, what would attract the world to our church?

What could we do to get the world inside our doors? And so, a great deal of effort has gone into making the church as comfortable as possible for the world. We want the man of the world to come into our services and be as comfortable as though he were born there. And the things that make a worldly person comfortable are amusements and entertainment. Whatever the world wants, we are prepared to give them.

If they do not like hymns, we will give them snappy little jingles they can whistle while they work.

If they do not like long expository sermons, we will give them little talks to help them on life's road.

If they want entertainment, well, it's entertainment we will give them.

If they do not want to think, we will amuse them to their little heart's content.

We now have almost perfected a feel-good religion that will not offend anybody. But I ask, whatever happened to the offense of the cross? Whatever happened to a separated life unto the Lord Jesus Christ in all purity and uprightness? Whatever happened to the stigma that honored the early Church?

## Self-Defense

Then, do not defend yourself and find an argument to make yourself look good. If you find that you cannot make time, stop and lay off that thing that is hindering you. Everyone knows his secret heart and all the reasons that can be given why a certain thing can be done. If it bothers you, then lay it off.

When we send up a rocket into space and start it around the earth, notice how smooth it is, how long and pointed and graceful.

It is made so there is nothing to catch the air and hold it back while it is getting out of the atmosphere. It has to be stream-lined so nothing will hold it back.

Someone can argue in favor of a thing and say, "It is good and cultural"; but if it bothers you, get rid of it. Do not waste your time, because if it prevents you from winning the race of life, you are far better to give it up.

## Peer Influence

To young Christians, I suppose this is the great universal en-cumbrance. It is great because young people are easily influ-enced; and it is universal because young people love to flock together. They are gregarious sheep, so unless they are ready to change friendships, let them wait and not say, "I accept the Lord," and then go back to old friendships. Some friendships you cannot keep and be a Christian.

I have found ways of getting rid of friends who are not go-ing in my direction. One is to talk to them so much about the Lord that you bore them stiff and they leave you on their own accord. That often happens. A new convert makes himself un-wanted by his constant talk about his newfound Christ. I think that is quite normal. But if some have tough hides and do not care how you talk and still insist on being with you and influ-encing you to do things you would not want to do and hear, and go to places you would not want to go of your own self, I say you had better break that friendship. A thousand times bet-ter to break a friendship than let it slow you down.

Any unspiritual friendship is like a great loose garment be-ing worn by a runner. In the old days it was called a toga, a great big old bathrobe affair that went around and tied around the waist by a belt. As long as you walked, you were all right; you did not notice the toga. But try to get up some speed and it would begin to flap in the breeze and hold you back. So the Greek runner did not wear his toga, he did not put on his top hat, he did not even wear the crown of laurel leaves he had won two weeks before. He put everything off except what decency required and raced along against the breeze with a streamlined human body. That is what the Holy Spirit says God's people must do. Friendships you cling to that cause your walk to flap in the breeze, that slow you down and hold you, you had better get rid of.

## Social Habits

These are habits about which there is not full agreement, but you know in your heart what they are and how they hinder you. The rebellious heart, of course, will resent interference into its social life. If there are social habits you cannot have and still be a Christian, at least a successful Christian, you need to break them off. Many of those habits that you used to have without any question before you were converted must now go. Christians cannot be too careful about their social habits.

## Reading Habits

Years ago, Jimmy Walker, the mayor of New York City, was called the Playboy Mayor and was always going about in coattails, silk hats and the rest of the attire. He was always around where society people were in all the nightclubs throughout New York City. Jimmy Walker was called one time as a witness about censoring books. On the stand, he tossed off a little quip and said, "I never heard of anybody ruined by reading a book." And of course the media grabbed that up and printed it all over the world. It was supposed to be very brilliant, but it was stupid, completely stupid.

Of course there have been people ruined by reading books. Maybe he did not have time in between cocktails to read up on it, but everybody knows what books do to people. Everybody knows what a Communist book will do to a young fellow in college if he gets hold of it, takes it home and reads it. Soon he has absorbed it and his eyes begin to blaze and he goes out to become a Communist.

Everybody knows how a humble, simple Christian, not too well informed in the Scripture, will get hold of a book written by Jehovah's Witnesses, falsely so-called, and read it and get all confused, and then buy another one and read it and have somebody in to talk. Soon he is out cursing the churches, denying the deity of Jesus, saying that the kingdom is coming and 144,000 will be saved, and all of this nonsense. He got it by reading a book.

On the other hand, I could tell stories by the hundreds of men who picked up a Christian tract or little book or picked up a Gideon Bible in a motel and were converted.

Our reading habits are important. The worldly wise will laugh, and the teachers and soft-voiced professors will recommend you become acquainted with all literature. They mean well, but they know not whereof they speak.

In my early life, I came to love a certain poet, an English translation of a very famous poem. It was on religion, philosophy, life, death and all the serious things but was not written by a Christian or by a man who knew God at all. It was brilliant and beautifully written, and the English translation was so beautiful, so musical, so smooth. I used to carry it around and memorize it. I can still repeat yards of it.

Later on, as I began to seek God in earnest, I began to see this book was a hindrance to me. If it did nothing else, it set a wrong mood of unbelief and pessimism instead of faith and hope. So I had it there on the shelf, four or five copies of it, and I did not look in it once in three years' time. I love it, it is brilliant poetry, its poetic music reminds me of Mozart, but I do not read it because it is a hindrance to me.

A university professor once heard me say I did not read Shakespeare anymore. He lamented the fact as if I had cancer or something seriously wrong with me.

I have not missed the old Bard of Avon; I look at him occasionally, but very rarely anymore, because I find not Christ in him. He was the greatest poet that ever lived, from the standpoint of literature. By the time you have wallowed through the suicides and murders and adulteries and betrayals and wars and assassinations and all the rest, even if it is classical, it is not good for you. So I just laid it aside. I would not say that no one ought to ever read it. If they give it to you in school, read it, find out what it is about, but do not make it your companion. I have a book here that is my constant companion. It is the Word of God.

## Personal Habits

Our personal habits would include the use of money, eating habits, general habits and dress. Somebody may object, "Now you are interfering; you're meddling in private affairs; it is none of your business." No, it is not any of my business, but it is an awful lot of you. You may laugh at me and say I am old-fashioned, but your personal habits will cause you to drag in your walk with Christ. Anything that makes your feet drag, preventing you from making time out there on the track, you had better get rid of it.

## Unblessed Plans

So many of the Lord's children have plans that God never gave them. They are not God-blessed plans. I have met men who at one time in their lives were happy Christians laboring with the church and on the board, leading singing, testifying. People looked to them as examples of what a Christian ought to be in life and in their business. Their business grew, and soon they had to miss prayer meeting to keep up with this new business; soon there was no glow in their countenance and no joy in their voice, and soon there was no willingness to testify. While they were still Christians, they were losing the race because they were allowing unblessed plans to hold them back. Better a hundred times to have less and have God than to have more and cloud the face of God.

The consequence of all these things would be to block the work of God in your heart and in your home and in your church. You cannot afford to do it. Time is too short. Judgment is too certain. Eternity is too long. God is too wonderful, and Christ is too beautiful, and heaven is too glorious for us to allow anything in our lives to hold us back from winning the race of life.

# Forth in Thy Name, O Lord, God
Charles Wesley (1707–1788)

Forth in Thy Name, O Lord, I go,
My daily labor to pursue;
Thee, only Thee, resolved to know
In all I think or speak or do.

The task Thy wisdom hath assigned,
O let me cheerfully fulfill;
In all my works Thy presence find,
And prove Thy good and perfect will.

Preserve me from my calling's snare,
And hide my simple heart above,
Above the thorns of choking care,
The gilded baits of worldly love.

Thee may I set at my right hand,
Whose eyes mine inmost substance see,
And labor on at Thy command,
And offer all my works to Thee.

Give me to bear Thy easy yoke,
And every moment watch and pray,
And still to things eternal look,
And hasten to Thy glorious day.

# 12

# WHAT TO DO WHEN FAITH FLAGS

*For consider him that endured such contradiction of sinners*
*against himself, lest ye be wearied and faint in your minds.*
*Ye have not yet resisted unto blood, striving against sin.*

HEBREWS 12:3-4

Many young converts are unsure of themselves and their faith, into which they have tentatively entered. They ask, in effect, just what is this Christian life, this saved life? How am I to learn how to live it? Who is to be my example and my model? How can I keep from wearing out and losing heart, ceasing to have any interest in it?

The answer, although simple enough, is "consider Him," think constantly of Jesus.

We get life from Jesus' dying and His resurrection, and we get courage to live by His having lived. It is the life He lived on earth that gives us encouragement and not the life He is now living in heaven. By knowing how He lived here, we can get the courage to persevere and keep on living. We can wear the devil out, get past all the obstacles, get over them, get around them, even if we become weary. We can lose that weariness or shut it off or endure it by knowing that Jesus was weary when He sat on the well in Samaria. And so we "consider Him," thinking constantly about the Lord Jesus Christ.

## Meditate for Life

To know how Jesus lived, we must read the Scriptures, learn them and then think upon what we have learned. I believe we ought to meditate three times more than we read. I believe that I can safely say that I think 10 times more than I ever read.

Dr. Samuel Johnson was invited by the king to come and have an evening with him. He was a well-known literary lion in those days, so he came over to the palace where the king lived, and they sat in front of the fireplace and talked. Finally, the king said, "I suppose, Doctor, that you have read a great deal."

Staring into the fire and thinking for a moment, Dr. Johnson said, "Yes, your Majesty, but I have thought more."

We ought to do a lot of thinking and meditating. I believe that if we were to meditate more, we would need to read less. This idea of speed-reading needs to be addressed, because what is the difference how many words went through your head if they did not leave any deposit there? What is the difference how many books you have read in the course of a week or a month if there was no result? I believe a little reading and a lot of reverent meditation will teach you more than you will ever learn from many books.

I once picked up the Apocrypha and noticed one sentence standing out. The gist of that sentence was that a man's own soul will sometimes give him more information than five watchmen on a watchtower. I did not read on. I do not know what that text had in mind, but I like that sort of thing. If you will stop, meditate and take the Word of God and dream over it and let it get hold of you, it will teach you more than you can learn from five watchmen on a watchtower.

So we are to meditate on, or consider, what happened to Jesus. Remember, Christians are Christ's younger brothers. He calls us brothers, and is not ashamed to address us by that name. He said that as He was sent into the world, so are we sent into the world, except, of course, there is one wonderful, lonely, isolated, glorious, unapproachable field where we cannot enter. When He went out to give Himself, the just for the unjust, the Lamb for sinners, and in the darkness of the cross did that mysterious something . . . whatever He did there in that act of redemption made it possible for God to justify sinners and forgive rebels and restore to His heart alienated men and women. We share not at all in that, and we can never share that. Our High Priest did that alone; but all the incidental living Christ did on earth we share as His younger brethren, and we go the way He went. He says that as He was in the world, so are we. He was the witness to things above, and so are we witnesses to things above.

My experience is more often that power lies in the little words than in the big ones. For example, the word "as" and the word "so" have tremendous power in them. Notice that in John 17:18, we read, "As thou hast sent me into the world, even so have I also sent them." "As thou has sent me," which was said of Jesus, and "so have I sent you," which is said of us. When the "so" becomes equal to the "as," then we are fulfilling the will of God. And then, "As he is, so are we in the world" (1 John 4:17).

A DISRUPTIVE FAITH

He was a witness on earth and a light to men; and we are to be the same. He was a moral judgment on the world, and so is every Christian a moral judgment on the world around us.

## Hostility by Another Name

I think it is one of the great mysteries of human life, this hostility of the world toward the Savior. He was rejected by His own nation, condemned by organized religion and executed by organized government. They did all of this without a cause. Jesus Himself said, "They hated me without a cause" (John 15:25).

There is such a thing of thinking up excuses for what you do. This is called rationalizing. You do what you do for a hidden reason, and then you give a plainly visible reason as the reason, which is not the reason at all. So anything they did against our Lord Jesus Christ was all rationalizing based on the hatred they felt for Him. They said, "He wants to be king!" What did they care about that? If He had become king and put down Caesar, they would have shouted and danced in the streets. They used that as an excuse, rationalizing their hatred for Christ.

But Jesus said, "I pray not for the world, but for them which thou hast given me; for they are thine" (John 17:9). Jesus did not give up His chosen individuals out of the world as lost, but He gave up the world as lost. "I pray not for the world" has bothered some people, but you find it there in the text of the prayer of Jesus.

You see, the prayer of Jesus is for His own people: "For I have given unto them the words which thou gavest me; and they have received them, and have known surely that I came out from thee, and they have believed that thou didst send me"

(John 17:8). These are those who are being prayed for by our High Priest and mediator at the right hand of God the Father. He does not expect the world to be anything. He implies that the world will get worse and worse, and evil men and seducers will even enter the church to such an extent that when the Son of Man comes, will He find faith on the earth? He expects the great world to rot and decay.

The world is rotting, it is decaying, and He expected it to be that way. But He has always had a people whom He has called out of the world. His elect, whom His soul delights in and whom He has called out, are His, and they are there from every tribe and nation and will be until the end comes.

## Christ's Freedom Incites Hostility

The world is hostile; and as a Christian, we live in a hostile environment. Keep that in mind. We are not playing on a field where everybody is friends with everybody else. We are fighting on the battleground where everybody on one side is the enemy to everybody on the other side. And there are two spirits in opposition to each other. Christ walked among men, inwardly free, and they said He broke the law. A Christian is, among other things, inwardly free.

One of the problems a pastor deals with is people with a morbid conscience. They are not free inside, so their conscience bothers them because they are breaking their own rules. The Jews, of course, were that kind of people. The Pharisees and the people in authority were that kind of people. Our Lord walked in the earth inwardly free, a perfectly free man. He was not going to sin, and God knew He was not going to sin, and Jesus knew God knew it. So whatever He did, He did not apologize for nor worry over. He just did it simply as a rose blooms quietly without any apology.

He just lived His inward life. The internal became the external, and what He was became what He did. He lived perfectly relaxed and not always digging at Himself and worrying about Himself. Of course, they said, He is a lawbreaker.

Here's an example. He and His disciples were going through the fields, and they had been on a long journey. The disciples were hungry and did what I have done as a boy a hundred times. They reached down, pulled the head off the wheat, rolled it in their hands, threshed it that way and then ate it. The Pharisees said, "Why are you threshing on the Sabbath?"

Can you imagine a thing like that on the Sabbath day? Can you imagine them objecting to anything as little as that? They objected because they were sick inside. Jesus and His disciples were free inside, and He was trying to make them free inside. He knew that the Lord God in heaven was not so hard to please and so pharisaical that He would care if a disciple reached down and pulled off a head of wheat and rolled it and got himself a mouthful to munch on as he continued his journey, waiting for a better dinner. That is why the free Christians have always been in trouble and have usually been called something else but free.

My good friend Tom Haire was having an all night of prayer. He frequently had all nights of prayer, two or three a week; but he had a group with him that night. Along about one o'clock or so, Tom, being an Irishman, suddenly wanted a cup of tea. Tom just got up, went out and made himself a cup of tea; the rest of them felt he was a sinner. They felt it was just terrible that this man would do such a thing. Why, he was supposed to be fasting, and he drank a cup of tea. The fact that he and God were on such good terms, I think God made the tea for him. He was perfectly free inside and did not worry.

## A Spotlight on Bondage

If you are in bondage to something, then you are in trouble with your conscience. But if you are free from everything and only in bondage to the love of God—a happy, joyful bondage to which you would not give up for the world—then whatever you do is all right because you do it in love.

Christ lived like that. Of course, that was contrary to the spirit of the world. The spirit of the world has no freedom in it, only bondage—to self, to sin, to the devil, to arbitrary moral rules and to religion that God had never given them. The result was, of course, they said, "He is a lawbreaker and he is leading the people astray." That brought the judgment on Him. And He walked familiarly with God; He talked about God as somebody He actually knew. He said, "Father, I thank thee that thou hast heard me" (John 11:41), and in John 1:8 we read, "The only begotten Son, which is in the bosom of the father." Jesus talked about the Father with the familiarity of a little boy talking about his father here on earth. I do not care how great the man is, his own son can never see it. His own son says, "He is just my dad," and they get wonderfully familiar in their conversation and talk.

The Father and the Son were in such perfect accord and so intimately related with a relaxed intimacy that the Lord Jesus Christ was perfectly free to do whatever came out of His heart to do. He knew He loved God and was living within the mighty, boundless framework of the revealed will of God. But the Pharisees could not see that. They had their own little rules. They added to the Ten Commandments over 365 other commandments. That would be one for every day; and then they put the pressure on for those other commandments to be just as great as the 10 God had given.

The Lord walked in that kind of world, surrounded by that kind of religion; He was a stranger to them and they to Him. Though He was one of them, born of the Virgin Mary, a Jew herself, still their religion separated them from Him because it was not arbitrarily created religious rules that the Lord lived by. He lived naturally out of a heart of love for His heavenly Father and for the world. They hated Him for that. And I say to you, the more carnal you are, the less trouble you will have with the world. The more spiritual you become, the more the world will persecute you for what you are.

Christ belongs to another world, and so does the Christian. We are brought out of the kingdom of darkness into the kingdom of the Son, and these two worlds can never be reconciled. This is one of the great basic truths you must know as a Christian, which if you fail to know, you will only have a social religious church—a religion that could not exist apart from its social activities. But if you see that the Christian belongs to another realm altogether, that he has been translated out of the kingdom of darkness and now exists in the kingdom of light, that he is here to mingle with and fellowship with others who have had the same experience, then you will see there is a different relationship held between the average religious church in the world and that held by the true Christian in the world.

## The Spiritual Man vs. the Religious Man

The spiritual man has treasures this world discounts. He has a mystic wisdom of the Holy Spirit, but the world has no way to receive this. Jesus said the world cannot receive him "because it seeth him not, neither knoweth him" (John 14:17). Just as a deaf man has no sensory organ to receive music, and just as a blind man has no organ to receive light, so a worldly man has no organ to receive the treasure of God's mystic knowledge by the Holy Spirit. And of course, if the Christian says he has and is sure of himself, the world is angry with him, even the religious world. They say he is a bigot, he thinks too much of himself. The Christian man has the Holy Spirit, invisible and from God, whom the world cannot receive. The Christian has heard a voice, seen the light and been able to repent and believe in the Lord Jesus Christ, while the world is just religious.

I am so deeply concerned that the evangelical fundamental church today should be a Christian church in every sense of the word. I am so deeply concerned that we should rise and shake off the grave clothes of dead denominational Christianity that lives on a dead tradition and runs like a truck with the engine off while the momentum carries it on. I am concerned that we should enter into the Christian life deeply, gravely, wonderfully, beautifully, and that we should be a people indwelt by the Holy Spirit, recognize ourselves as a minority group living in a world that hated our Lord and hates us for our Lord's sake. If we act like our Lord, He adopts us and accepts us and uses us, if we do not reject Him.

The way I keep from being weary in my Christian life is to remember what I am here for. I am here to endure trouble. I am here to endure the friction the world gives. As my Lord was in this world, so am I. He was rejected, and so will I be. He was hated, and so will I be. The world did not understand Him, and they will not understand me.

Somebody might object and say, "You're gloomy. This is terrible." We are living in a time when we have to be chucked up, cheered up. Let me give you the rest of the story: "Wherefore God also hath highly exalted him, and given him a name which is above every name: That at the name of Jesus every knee should bow, of things in heaven, and things in earth, and things under the earth; and that every tongue should confess that Jesus Christ is Lord, to the glory of God the Father" (Phil. 2:9-11).

He had to brace Himself and throw off the weariness of living in a world that hated Him. He had to continue to live in it until He went down as far as He could go; and when He was down as far as He could get, then God reversed Him and up He came as far as He could come, even to the right hand of God the Father, with every knee bowing and every tongue confessing in heaven, earth and hell that He is Lord to the glory of God the Father.

Dear Christian, as He was, so are we in this world. We are called to follow Him through earth's hardships, in light labors, through the struggles and disappointments and grief and rejection; and when He finds that we have had enough of it, He will bring us up into a place of glorious power and light and usefulness even in this world. Of course, ultimately the final glory is in the world to come. May God help us now to work and not be weary, because there is full reward coming for all of the Lord's overcoming saints.

## Am I a Soldier of the Cross?
Isaac Watts (1674–1748)

Am I a solder of the Cross,
A foll'wer of the Lamb,
And shall I fear to own
His cause or blush to speak His name?

Must I be carried to the skies
On flow'ry beds of ease
While others fought to win the prize
And sailed thro' bloody seas?

Are there no foes for me to face?
Must I not stem the flood?
Is this vile world a friend to grace
To help me on to God?

Sure I must fight if I would reign;
Increase my courage, Lord!
I'll bear the toil, endure the pain,
Supported by Thy Word.

Thy saints in all this glorious war
Shall conquer though they die;
They see the triumph from afar
With faith's discerning eye.

When that illustrious Day shall rise
And all Thine armies shine
In robes of victory through the skies,
The glory shall be Thine.

# 13

# THE ULTIMATE GOAL OF OUR FAITH

*Now no chastening for the present seemeth to be joyous,*
*but grievous: nevertheless afterward it yieldeth the peaceable fruit*
*of righteousness unto them which are exercised thereby.*

HEBREWS 12:11

To a great degree, Christian discipleship has been a neglected doctrine in this generation. Few people want to hear anything much about discipleship. Our great emphasis now is not on being a disciple of Christ, but on just getting through "by the skin of your teeth" by believing in Christ. I do not want to underestimate the message of believing on the Lord Jesus Christ. That is basic to our life as a Christian, and apart from this, we have no message.

Once a person has believed on the Lord Jesus Christ, however, a great new and wonderful life opens up for him. This is where many sink into a theological quagmire. The emphasis is so much on "believe on the Lord Jesus Christ," but nothing else really gets through. Just "get saved," and everything else is okay. The implication is that you can go back and live the life you lived before. But where is the change? Where is a life that is absolutely committed to the Lord Jesus Christ?

Allow me to point out something that may sound a little shocking. It is simply this: *It is an error for anybody to assume that to be saved is to be automatically ready for heaven.* I know this may fall crossways across your thinking.

Let me use an illustration that will emphasize what I'm trying to say here. Take that newborn baby the expectant mother and father have been waiting for at least nine months. The day has arrived when their first baby comes bouncing into the world. What a wonderful occasion that is. My wife and I had seven children, and I know the extreme excitement of that new little baby coming into the home.

What do the parents do after that baby arrives?

"Okay, Junior," the father says to the child, "you have been here in our home for a whole week now, and I think it's about time you went out and started to earn your living." What a rather silly thing for any father to say.

Although that young child is 100 percent human, no doubt about that, it is in no shape to face the world. It cannot go out, get a job and make a living. It is not equipped for that. I am in no way demeaning the humanness of that little baby. What I'm trying to point out is simply that the child is not prepared to take on the world.

In a similar vein, that person just coming to Jesus Christ, who has believed on Jesus as his Savior, is 100 percent Christian, but he or she is not quite ready for heaven. There is a lifetime of discipleship ahead of that new Christian, preparing him for the world to come.

Somebody might stop me here and remind me of the thief on the cross. Or somebody else might remind me of a loved one who prayed to accept Jesus Christ as their Savior on their deathbed and a few hours later they died. What about these people?

Certainly, anybody who calls upon the name of the Lord Jesus Christ, the Bible tells us, shall be saved. And certainly when the thief on the cross put his trust in Jesus, not knowing all the little things about Jesus, he was saved. And that deathbed confession is as genuine as it could possibly be. But let me point out that these are the exceptions.

It is not in God's plan for a person to get to heaven by the skin of his teeth. I'm sure many will, but the plan of God is for us to become a Christian and then through discipleship become all God wants us to be in this life. The old preachers of another generation used to preach that this life was preparation and rehearsal for the life to come. Growth and development in our Christian life is absolutely essential to prepare us for heaven.

## Salvation Is Just the Beginning

This discipleship is an ongoing thing with progressive stages to it.

When you begin with the little baby, you do not start teaching him Einstein's theory of relativity. You begin with the very basics and then build on that. When that baby is ready to go to school, he starts at the first grade, not the ninth grade. He goes from first grade to second grade to third grade all the way up until he graduates from high school. There is progressiveness to this matter of discipleship.

The new Christian begins with the very basics and then builds up step by step into the deeper things of God unto full Sonship.

Discipleship is dealt with in Hebrews 12. If the moment we were converted we were ready for heaven and ready for the future and ready for everything, we would instantly be taken to heaven with nothing in between. But the truth is simply that we are not ready. Theologically, so to speak, we are ready because we have eternal life. But to say that the new believer can be up on the level with the heroes of the Lion's den and the fiery furnace and the gallows and the martyrs who were burned at the stake is to misunderstand the whole plan of God.

Evangelical fundamentalist Christianity is in the mess it is in today because we preach a painless and instant Christianity. All you do is pour hot water on it, stir twice, take a tract and go your way. As soon as a person is saved, he is automatically everything he should be. Give him a handful of tracts and send him out into the world and say, "Go and evangelize the world."

I'm for evangelizing the world, all right. But we need to rethink some of this that we're doing these days. Christianity is not the automatic thing that so many people are advocating. Maybe that is why evangelism is not the high priority among so many churches today.

Some are out trying to do the Lord's work and have not the slightest idea of what that work is supposed to be. Consequently, whole groups of Christians are borrowing their ideas from the world. They simply have not been taught the Bible way of doing things. Someone becomes a Christian right out of the world and doesn't know any better, so he uses what he used to use out in the world to try to advance the kingdom of God. It never works.

What we end up with is simply large segments of the evangelical fundamentalist church today infected with mediocre spirituality; some of the Bible mixed in with some of the world, and there you have the average church today.

I believe in democracy all right. I believe it is the best form of government yet; and I would not want to see any of the democratic countries change to any other form of government, but it is a long way from being perfect.

A man will spend his whole year working, fishing, washing his car, looking at television, playing golf and not even listen to the news or read up enough to know the name of his senator who represents him, and could not name him if he were lined up against a wall to be shot. Then when voting time comes, he squares his shoulders, heaves out his chest and starts for the polls. Just as well prepared to vote as a Hottentot. That is democracy. It is not democracy as it ought to be or as it could be or should be. But it is true to a tragic degree. Then, totally unprepared men decide how things are to go; thus we have a democracy of the mediocre, a paradise for the ordinary.

Heaven above is not going to be anything like that. Grace makes us equal before the law, but it does not obliterate distinctions; it does not put crowns on empty heads; it does not guarantee rewards to the undeserving. God regards the obedience, sacrifice, faithfulness, suffering service and motives, taking them all into account in preparing His people and giving rewards later at the consummation of all things.

What many people overlook in the kingdom of God is God's high expectation for humanity. God did not create us and then turn His back on us; He did not leave us purposeless in a meaningless world. No, God has a marvelous plan for each of us; and according to the plan, God is preparing us here and now on earth.

In order for us to understand what God has in store for each and every one of us, we need to understand a little more about God Himself. This is why we cannot believe in evolution. God did not just wind up creation and then let it go its own way. Behind every creative act of God is a purpose born in His heart of love and grace. To miss this is to misunderstand the high and holy purpose God has for each and every person.

The purpose of God for every person was destroyed the day Adam and Eve sinned. The fall of man introduced into humanity a depravity that robbed God of His intention for men and women. We sometimes think of sin from man's side of it. But think a little bit of what sin did for God. It robbed God of His ultimate purpose in creation. Man had holy purposes assigned to him at creation.

## Wild Colts and Wandering Sheep

It was redemption that brought man back into that place of God's purpose. Once a person is born again, he enters into this lifestyle full of God's purpose. That purpose is uncovered step by step as we give ourselves to holy discipleship, which includes obedience to the Word and to the will of God.

God knows that even after we are converted and have a new nature planted within us, we are still more or less sons and daughters of the wild ass's colt, as Job would put it. And there is a wild, untamed spirit within us that has to be disciplined and brought into line and taught. There is basic ignorance in us amounting to genius that God has to instruct. There is pigheadedness that God has to break, tame and discipline. There is laziness in us that God has to stir up. There is self-love that

God has to crucify. Then He has to teach us to obey. That thing our father refused to do, sinned and fell. In Adam's fall, we all fell. And we all got that indisposition to obey.

I come from a family where they considered obedience to be for weaklings and sissies. My father was such an independent man that when he left the farm and got a job in a rubber factory, he considered himself insulted if a foreman told him what to do. He did not want to be bossed around by any foreman. Who was that fellow to tell him? He was being paid to do a certain work and did not want to know what it was. I do not excuse that. I just say that is an extreme case of the independent individualism gone wild.

We have in our modern day untamed, unbroken colts of the pasture field; we call them Christians. If they do not like a pastor, they run across the street and join another church. If they do not like something that pastor does, they go two blocks down and join another one; and if they do not like that, they go across the street, rent a barbershop, start one of their own. The result is that we have untamed, unbroken colts of the pasture who have never known the feel of the yoke with a harness. If I were to use a more biblical image, we have sheep that know not their master's voice and are victims to the voices of strangers who only want their wool.

Our Lord calls us to discipleship, to be a disciple of the cross. "If any man will come after me, let him deny himself, and take up his cross" (Matt. 16:24). But you know, it is not so hard, for His yoke is easy and His burden is light (see Matt. 11:30).

God has His rod, certainly, but that is a bad figure of speech and does not have the same meaning regarding the Shepherd as it does in the household. But if we are without chastisement, then we are not true children of the Father. He said that if you want the Father to own you as His child, and look after you as His child, you need to yield to His discipline. He explains how we have fathers in the flesh; then He explains that no chastening ever seems joyous at the time.

## The Peaceable Fruit of Discipline

Years ago, there was a dear old preacher, now in heaven: Buddy Robinson, affectionately called Buddy by everybody. He was one of the great preachers of his day. He once said his mother was one of the most patriotic woman he ever knew. He said that when he did something wrong, his mother took him over her knee and he saw stars. Then he said, not only that, but when she was finished, he was red, white and blue.

Well, that kind of discipline can be overdone, but it did something for Buddy, all right. He became one of the world's great preachers. Nobody likes it when seeing the stars, but afterward the end result is the peaceable fruit of righteousness.

It is wonderful to think of the peaceable fruit of righteousness. Many have wrong ideas of what discipleship is all about. Perhaps it goes back to our relationship to our father. Maybe we thought he disciplined us too harshly. Maybe he did. But God's discipline flows from a heart of love. God will never do anything in a believer's life that will destroy his or her joy. Destruction is the job of the world, the flesh and the devil.

Discipleship from God's point of view is simply to bring our lives into harmony with His life. The entire Godhead—God the Father, God the Son, and God the Holy Spirit—is in complete agreement with this harmony. And what God wants to do is to bring you into that harmony of the Godhead that already exists.

I pray that somehow, some way in this generation, there might be a revival of biblical discipleship. That God's people may understand they are children in the Father's house, learning down here how to live over there.

## This World Is Not My Home
Albert Edward Brumley (1905–1977)

This world is not my home, I'm just passing through.
My treasures are laid up somewhere beyond the blue.
The angels beckon me from Heaven's open door
And I can't feel at home in this world anymore.

They're all expecting me and that's one thing I know.
My Savior pardoned me and now I onward go.
I know He'll take me through, though I am weak and poor
And I can't feel at home in this world anymore.

Just up in Glory Land we'll live eternally.
The Saints on every hand are shouting victory.
Their song of sweetest praise drifts back from Heaven's shore
And I can't feel at home in this world anymore.

O Lord you know I have no friend like you
If Heaven's not my home, then Lord what will I do?
The angels beckon me from Heaven's open door
And I can't feel at home in this world anymore.

# 14

# THE HOLY NATURE OF OUR FAITH

*Follow peace with all men, and holiness,*
*without which no man shall see the Lord.*

HEBREWS 12:14

The Bible specifically commands us to follow holiness. It is to be our constant ambition. One way to advance in this pursuit of holiness is to accept chastisement and work with God as God works in us.

Holiness is godlikeness, for only God is absolutely holy. All other holy beings are holy in relative degrees. Scripture tells us of the holy angels who will come with Jesus; but even those holy angels have their holiness from another source; it is not native to them. They reflect the glory of God, and that is their holiness. We learn also that holy men of God spoke as the Holy Spirit moved them. Though the word "holy" is the same, for the Holy Spirit it means absolute, uncreated holiness. For the holy man who spoke, it means a derived holiness that comes from God.

God said, "Be ye holy; for I am holy" (1 Pet. 1:16). I am so glad He did not say, "Be ye holy as I am holy," for this would be one of the most impossible, discouraging, disheartening commandments possible. The focus is, be ye getting holy, becoming holy and relative holy, because I am absolute holiness. What does "holy" mean? As I see it, "holy" has two aspects to it. It has what someone called the numinous quality, and then it has the moral quality.

## The Numinous Quality of Holiness

By numinous, we mean God exists in Himself; God's being is. He says, "I am that I am." His nature is inconceivable; we cannot lay hold of it with our mind at all. This is sound Bible doctrine.

When I have had occasion to mention the incomprehensibility of God, some people have raised objections as though I were a heretic fresh out of Rome or somewhere. In fact, the theologians have taught the incomprehensibility of God from the apostle Paul all the way down to this present hour—deep theologians who knew what they were teaching. Therefore, God cannot be comprehended. And not being able to comprehend Him, we cannot speak Him forth. So He is said to be ineffable. "Ineffable" means you cannot speak it; and if you cannot know it you cannot speak it.

Then the nature of God is unique. God is of a substance not shared by any other being, hence He can only be known as He chooses to reveal Himself. God must reveal Himself, because man could not know Him otherwise. It takes similarities to know each other; and because God is not similar to any other things, but rather unique beyond all creaturehood, He has to reveal Himself.

God's nature is also supernatural. That is, we cannot comprehend it with our minds. It is unearthly, otherworldly; it is beyond all human understanding. Yet it is not beyond experiencing. Even though all this is true of God, God can yet make Himself known to us. He can manifest Himself to people, and He did just that to the people in Old Testament times.

He saw Adam and Eve in the Garden, in the cool of the day, while they hid among the trees in their fear. Every time God thus manifested Himself to them, they did not try to understand God, but rather, to experience Him. Every time this incomprehensible, inconceivable, ineffable and utterly holy God made Himself known to anybody, immediately their mouths were shut and they fell down in a dead faint or ran and hid or cried, "My God, I am unclean" (see Isa. 6:5). Or they otherwise expressed the reaction of one undone in the presence of this holy God. It brought dismay to their hearts, inspired terror, stupefied and appalled them.

It seems to me this is what is lacking in our church today and in most evangelical churches. Everybody can predict everything; everybody comes completely self-possessed and knows exactly what is going to happen. You could not, unless the church caught fire, bump anybody to do anything that was not proper.

I pray that God may sometime move in on us in such a way that it will have the effect it had on Abraham when a deep sleep fell upon him in the horror of great darkness (see Gen. 15:12). That God would move in on us so that it will have the effect on us that it had on Moses when he shook with exceeding fear (see Heb. 12:21). And on Ezekiel when he fell down upon his face (see Ezek. 11:13), and when Paul was struck blind on the road to Damascus, where he was speechless and went without food because he had seen the awful, wondrous, lovely God he heard about but had not seen before this (see Acts 9:3-9).

The Lord picked up the apostle John and said, "Fear not; I am the first and the last: I am he that liveth, and was dead; and, behold, I am alive for evermore" (Rev. 1:17-18). He knew John could not help it. When John, being a sinful creature, met this uncreated holiness that manifested itself, it fell on John as though he had been struck with the blow of a hammer. The Lord did not condemn his reaction; He understood. He knew it was John's weakness reacting to His strength, John's unholiness reacting to God's awesome holiness.

In the New Testament, wherever the Spirit fell, there came this strange sense of the mysterious working of the supernatural; this sense of the previously unfamiliar presence. This wondrous, ineffable presence was unearthly. In the book of Corinthians, Paul admits that even though the Corinthian church was not all it should be, yet there were those among them who were spiritual enough to form the nucleus that the Holy Spirit could come upon. Men who were not Christians fell on their faces and said, "God is among us of a truth."

This, I say, is what we need today.

What is the reaction of the cleansed heart, the loving heart? It is to find this blissful center around which we revolve. Nothing can truly equal the life of the Christian. It is the most wondrous and desirable life to be found anywhere. The Christian is surrounded with the poetry of God's majesty and holiness. God's presence whispers deep into the heart of the believer like David's fingers on his harp. It is a life surrounded by the manifest presence of God.

Today, however, we have a different idea about this. I can truthfully say this is the day of the absentee God. At least, many of God's people act as though God were on vacation somewhere. And for the most part, this does not really bother the average Christian, for the simple reason that if God is not really present, He does not put too much demand on us. It's almost like an employee who takes great pleasure in the absence of his boss, knowing that he can get away with things behind the boss's back.

On occasion, when the average Christian needs something from God, he begins looking around for God. If you have to look around for God, something is wrong. God is not lost. God is not on vacation. God is not absent from our life. If we live as though God is not present in our life, we are not living the kind of Christian life God has designed for us.

One of the most ridiculous applications of this is seen in the fact that groups of Christians get together as a committee and try to figure out how to do God's work. The simple truth is, my friend, nobody can do God's work. Only God can do God's work. And God is looking for that humble Christian who has so cultivated the presence of God that the work of God flows naturally through him or her. The presence of God is beautiful and desirable to the cleansed, loving heart of the believer.

## The Moral Quality of Holiness

Then we have the holiness of God. The holiness of God is the moral quality of God. This is a little more familiar, a little more understandable and not quite so terrifying to the soul. We are drawn as Christians to that which is pure. God's nature is unspeakably pure, sinless, spotless, immaculate, stainless and with an absolute fullness of purity that words can never express. God is a holy God; you can always be sure God is all right. That can be at the very bottom basis of all your thinking about God—God is all right, God is holy, God is pure.

I remember that wondrous passage in Psalm 22, referring to when our Lord Jesus hung on the cross. His family had deserted Him. His disciples had fled away. His own people had condemned Him to death. The Romans had officially executed Him. He was crucified, rejected of men and He died—the just for the unjust—that He might bring us back to God. In that awful hour, when the Bulls of Bashan were crowding around Him and His tongue was cleaving to the roof of His mouth and His bones were out of joint and His life was being poured out like water, what could He do?

Could He turn atheist there on the cross? Could He begin to condemn God and say, "I cannot believe there is a God who would do this"? No. He did this one awful, wonderful, lonely, beautiful thing there on the cross. He lifted His voice and said, "Father, into thy hands I commend my spirit" (Luke 23:46). He recognized that "thou art holy, O thou that inhabitest the praises of Israel" (Ps. 22:3). If they tore Him to pieces, trampled His body into the ground, subjected Him to every torture known to humanity, still, He knew one thing: God is holy and cannot be anything else but holy. Here, not John 3:16, is the basic pillar upon which Christianity rests. It is God is holy, and everything God does and all of the beautiful things of the New Testament spring out of the great fountain of truth that God is holy.

God's nature is unspeakably pure, and this has affected men. It drove Peter to quick confession: "Depart from me; for I am a sinful man, O Lord" (Luke 5:8). Isaiah cried, "I am undone; because I am a man of unclean lips" (Isa. 6:5). It is this kind of holiness, the moral quality, that would die rather than do wrong. It is settled forever and ever that we will be right because God is right. We will be holy because God is holy. It is this that we are to pursue, to know, to entertain, to dwell in the divine.

Today the poor evangelical fundamental church is being taken to the halls of so-called learning, and their Christianity is being mingled and mixed with anthropology and psychology. Both are now used to dilute and water down and change the whole complexion of the Christian life. And they can explain the Lord's people now, which is the greatest insult to us as believers. When God has a people back again in the world that cannot be explained, He will have a people with power.

D. L. Moody, the great American evangelist, went to an English city and visited the Atheist Club. Moody had no formal education; he was converted as a boy off the streets of Boston. He announced that he was going to preach to the atheist, and everyone thought it was a big joke. The president of the club and other members, officers along with their members, all turned out that night. Moody took for his text a verse that I do not think he understood. I have not met anybody that really did understand it, but he used it: "For their rock is not as our Rock, even our enemies themselves being judges" (Deut. 32:31). What that means I am not really sure, but Moody preached on it.

Here's how Moody applied this verse: "Whatever rock you are resting on is not like our rock, and we let you be the judge. Your little rock, your little sandstone rock that you perch on there like a toad on a water pad, there you are, but your rock will crumble; but our rock is not like your rock. Our rock will last, the rock of ages. Now you be the judge."

I do not think I could have got that out of that verse, but Moody did. When he gave the invitation, the president of the Atheist Club, not being argued into it but brought into it by the presence of the mysterious, awful God in their midst, went in the inquiry room. And as soon as he had broken the ice, the others trekked in and the whole club was converted and broke up and went out of business. Psychologists cannot explain that; that was God.

People are always talking about creatures from other places, extraterrestrial creatures invading our planet. What we need is to have creatures from other worlds born down here, but their citizenship is in heaven. All their thoughts are in heaven. Their hopes are there, their power is there. When they were born again, they became creatures from another world. It is this we need, and this will do more than all our other attempts to explain through psychology what happens when a man is converted. If you can explain it, he has not been converted. Christianity is a perpetual miracle. It is a miracle that perpetuates itself, a continuous wonder and mystery. Yet we walk sanely in the midst of it with our feet on the ground.

If anybody rejects this, then he or she is not His. Just as a natural baby born into the world wants its food and will make funny little animal noises and call after the food until he gets it, so too a man born into the kingdom of God is born with an instinct after holiness; and if he does not have it, he has not been born again. His theological background may be such that he would be cautious about the Word because his fingers may have been burnt, but if you are not longing to be holy, then I doubt whether you have been born anew.

## Jesus, Think All Victorious Love
Charles Wesley (1707–1788)

Jesus, Thine all victorious love
Shed in my heart abroad;
Then shall my feet no longer rove,
Rooted and fixed in God.

O that in me the sacred fire
Might now begin to glow;
Burn up the dross of base desire
And make the mountains flow!

O that it now from Heav'n might fall
And all my sins consume!
Come, Holy Ghost, for Thee I call,
Spirit of burning, come!

Refining fire, go through my heart,
Illuminate my soul;
Scatter Thy life through every part
And sanctify the whole.

# 15

# THE HIDDEN LIFE OF FAITH

*And it shall come to pass, while my glory passeth by, that I will put thee*
*in a clift of the rock, and will cover thee with my hand while I pass by.*

EXODUS 33:22

This Scripture describes one of the most charming and beautiful scenes found anywhere in the entire Bible. I would not say it
is a type of anything, but I would say that it is a marvelously
beautiful illustration. It does not so much preach to us as it
sings to us, and it sings to us the song of the hidden life. It is
the hidden life of faith, the song of the man Moses, who found
a hiding place in the smitten rock.

The gospel Oracle has certain clear, specific results. The
foundation of those results is faith in God. Right here is where
many flounder. It is not that we do not believe in faith, rather
we have de-emphasized it to such a degree that it is no longer a
valid doctrine among many Christians. Some believe that faith
is simply a conclusion drawn from the facts. Any faith that we
achieve on our own is simply not biblical faith.

Unless we understand that Bible faith is an impartation by
the Holy Spirit to the believing and obedient heart, it remains
inoperative. Just because something is stated in the Scriptures

does not make it a reality in my heart. Anybody can line up a string of Bible texts and then draw a conclusion that it is part of our life. It can be, but unless there is an operation of the Holy Spirit in our contrite heart, those Scriptures remain just a series of Bible texts.

Faith in the gospel Oracle for man is a gift of God, the spiritual ability to trust Christ by the Holy Spirit through the penitent man, and this faith is withheld from every other sort of man. This imparted faith enters an immortal Kingdom at once. The man of faith comes into the kingdom of God and joins a select circle, the elect. It is not the ecumenical circle that we hear about so much. It is more than that. It is the elect, God's kingdom. And when a man enters that Kingdom, he becomes what I call "God's hidden man." "I will hide thee," said God. "I will put thee in a cleft of the rock."

Let me outline several features of this man of faith.

## The God-Charmed Man

The first I might say is that he is a God-charmed man. I am aware that many people have wrongly taught this. This God-charmed man lives in the center of a miracle and he becomes, in one real sense, a true Bible mystic. He feels the whole world is his and he comes into accord with it.

For the God-charmed man, nothing in this world can in the least way compromise his life. Although all the gates of hell may be arrayed against him, there is a tranquility that rises above any hostile circumstances. Read the lives of the saints. Read the lives of those who were martyred for the cause of Christ. Although these lived in circumstances so very hostile to them that it cost them their lives, they were living in the center of a miracle that nothing on the outside could ever touch.

Wherever a Christian may find himself, and whatever those circumstances might be, nothing can touch him. In the Old Testament, Job was a God-charmed man. When Satan wanted to touch Job, he complained to God, "Hast not thou made an hedge about him, and about his house, and about all that he hath on every side? Thou hast blessed the work of his hands, and his substance is increased in the land" (Job 1:10).

This God-charmed man sees the miracle where everybody else does not see a miracle at all. He sees the clash of the laws of nature and matter and form; the true child of God sees the miracle. It is not a sign of senility or a sign that a man's mind is bad when he insists upon seeing God in a grain of sand and on hearing the voice of God in the sighing of the wind or in the roar of the storm.

It was said about Jesus, you remember, that His hour was not yet come. They could harm Him while He walked among them, because His hour was not yet come. He was a God-charmed man.

The Old Testament is full of such examples of the God-charmed life. Name any of the prophets and you will find they lived the God-charmed life.

Elijah is one example. Just when the king thought he had him surrounded, Elijah disappeared. The king could only get to Elijah when God wanted him to. And the blessed thing about this is Elijah knew that as well. He lived a God-charmed life in the midst of hostilities. No matter if he was facing the fury of the king or standing next to a stream that had just dried up,

Elijah feared no evil, for he knew God was with him.

And what about David? Before ascending to the throne, he was hunted like an animal by King Saul. What King Saul did not understand was that David was living a God-charmed life. No matter how close Saul came to capturing David, he could never touch him. The stories surrounding David's life during this time are amazing to read. No matter where David was, as long as he was where God wanted him to be, nobody could touch him. It was David who wrote, "Yea, though I walk through the valley of the shadow of death, I will fear no evil: for thou art with me; thy rod and thy staff they comfort me" (Ps. 23:4).

Daniel was another case of a God-charmed man. Even when the whole court was against him, he never feared and never compromised his walk with God. When the judgment came against him and he was sentenced to the lions' den, Daniel understood that standing between him and all those ferocious lions was the God he served. Facing those lions, Daniel had a tranquil heart because he understood what it meant to live a God-charmed life.

I have many examples drawn from Church history that could be given in proof of the fact of the God-charmed life. If a man obeys God, he cannot die until his work is done. He is a God-charmed man. Now, if that man leaves the way and goes among the wolves of his own intention, I have no hope then that he shall ever fulfill the will of God. But if he obeys and goes where God sends him, he is a safe man until he is ready to die; and who wants to live five minutes after the Lord says, "Come up here"?

## The God-Defended Man

This man of faith is not only a God-charmed man with a charmed life, but he is also a God-defended man.

I get a lot of help from Moses. When Moses was in a jam with the people of Israel, or somebody was after him, it says in solemn language, "And it came to pass, as Moses entered into the tabernacle, the cloudy pillar descended, and stood at the door of the tabernacle, and the Lord talked with Moses" (Exod. 33:9). Moses stood back behind, and the angry murderous men and women surrounding him withdrew. When the woodsman built a huge roaring fire, you could see their eyes shining in the dark, but not one dared come through the circle of light.

The Scriptures are filled with this kind of admonition: "No weapon that is formed against thee shall prosper; and every tongue that shall rise against thee in judgment thou shalt condemn. This is the heritage of the servants of the LORD, and their righteousness is of me, saith the LORD" (Isa. 54:17). If there is a tongue that rises against you, is it a true tongue about you? The Lord will not condemn that tongue; but if it is not true, then the Lord will condemn that tongue. He says, "I will go before thee."

One of the greatest preachers I have ever heard was a Southerner from North Carolina by the name of L. D. Compton. If this man's experiences were written up in the slow, stately language of the *King James*, it might well be misunderstood as a lost chapter from the New Testament. Once, a rich townsman sued him for something for which he was not to blame, but the influence was on the side of the rich man. People asked him, "Why don't you get your witnesses and do something?" All he would say was, "I cannot. God will not let me. All God will let me do is pray." So he prayed down to the wire.

The day before the suit was to be held in court, and everybody knew that a poor preacher did not stand a chance against an influential townsman who had brought the suit against him, the man of God waited on God in holy prayer. And the day of the trial came. A few hours before the trial was to begin, the preacher got a call. "Please come down and pray for a man who is desperately ill."

He hurried down, and you guessed it, the ill man was the man who was suing him in court. The preacher got down on his knees beside the bed and prayed for the man's healing, and the man was instantly healed. The rich man got up, called off the suit and everybody said, "What hath God wrought?"

When a man defends himself, he has only his self for his defense. But the man who allows God to be his defense has all of the resources of heaven at his disposal.

When a man belongs to this God-charmed circle, he is also a God-defended man.

## The God-Taught Man

In 1 Corinthians 2:7, Paul says, "But we speak the wisdom of God in a mystery, even the hidden wisdom, which God ordained before the world unto our glory." Let me illustrate this by a testimony I once heard. A good brother, by the name of Olson, a man without much education, but a deeply spiritual man of God, shared his testimony. When he was a young preacher, he had a radio ministry in the local community. One day he got a call: "Would you please come out to such and such a place, just outside of town and have a little meeting with us there?"

So, not thinking too much of it, he took his guitar and hymnbooks and a friend and they drove out to where the meeting was supposed to be. The yard was full of cars and the house was full of people. People were sitting around on chairs, and when he walked in, they looked at him as if he was a stranger. But God had sent him, so he passed the hymnbooks around, got the key on his guitar and began to sing.

He then asked his friend to testify, which he did. Then he launched into a solid gospel sermon. He gave the altar call and everybody went down on their knees and began to pray, and many of them found Christ. As he was gathering up his hymnbooks and started for the car, someone ran out and said, "Brother Olson, come back and pray for my sick sister." Brother Olson said, "Are you and your sister saved?" When the answer was in the negative, he said, "You both will get saved before I will pray for her to be healed."

He led them to Christ, and as far as he knows, a large number of those who were saved that day were still walking with God years later. When he had gotten safely away from the home, and the circumstances were known, he found that he was in the wrong house; it was a family reunion of the Nelson clan and nobody there was expecting him.

That is what I mean by a God-taught man. Here was a simple-hearted man that would not know a Greek root from a root of ginseng, but he did know the voice of God when he heard it. The Lord had had His way with a man who was simple enough to listen to God speak and minister to his heart. A man that is hidden is a God-taught man without a doubt, because he is led by a kind of spiritual instinct if he is a prayerful man.

I read not long ago of a female dog that had been around the place and was loved by all, but something happened and they sold her. They took her 3,000 miles across the continent and forgot about her. Twenty-one days later, she came limping in, the pads of her feet were bleeding and she herself was a complete wreck and nothing but skin and bones. But she carried her nose across the threshold and lay down and looked up and whimpered. She was back home. How did she find her way home through the unknown highways of thousands of miles? Nobody can tell you that.

In Russia, when a man is lost, he does not try to find his way home. Instead, he simply speaks to his horse, lets the reins loose and braces himself against the storm, and the horse finds her way home. In the same way, the swallow finds its way back from San Juan Capistrano, and nobody knows how. There is a spiritual instinct that is like that. You are puzzled, you comb your intellect but nothing registers. No bells ring. You make a decision, and after a few years have gone by it turns out to be the right thing. Why did you do the right thing? There is a hidden mystery, which is ordained before the foundation of the world.

God is speaking, and there is a mysterious wisdom moving among men, and God is saying, "If you do not get right, you will rattle yourself to death." When He is beginning to give life back to us again, and if the Lord lets some of us live a little while longer and keep on going, I believe the day will come when we will get away from Hollywood and away from the hard dispensationalism and back to the charmed life, the Spirit-filled life, the God-blessed life.

## The God-Fed Man

An important aspect of this man of faith is that he is a God-fed man. "He that hath an ear, let him hear what the Spirit saith unto the churches; to him that overcometh will I give to eat of the hidden manna, and will give him a white stone, and in the stone a new name written, which no man knoweth saving he that receiveth it" (Rev. 2:17).

This God-fed man is completely dependent upon the Holy Spirit for his nourishment and strength. He regularly feeds upon the "hidden manna" provided for him by God. Remember Elijah, by the stream where the ravens came every day to feed him? Then when the stream dried up because of the drought, God sent him to a widow woman who did not know she had the means to feed her and her son, let alone bless anybody else. She was, however, appointed by God to feed his man Elijah.

We need that "hidden manna" today if we are going to have the strength to do what God wants us to do. But that "hidden manna" only comes to the man who is where God wants him to be. Had Elijah stayed by the stream he would have died of hunger. But in obedience he went where God wanted him to go and was a God-fed man.

## The God-Privileged Man

The man of faith is a man of mystery who lives under the hand of God and lives a life too pure for the flesh to analyze. Not all of the psychiatrists or psychoanalysts in the world can ever figure out or understand this man of faith. They may be able to understand the mind and how the mind works, but they will never understand how the spirit, indwelt by the Holy Spirit, works and moves in this world of ours. They cannot analyze the man of faith because the man of faith lives in the mystery.

The God-privileged man walks in a mystery, even to himself. Reason is not king for the God-privileged man. Often the man of faith will be led to do those things that do not on the surface look very reasonable. But the walk of faith brings us into an aura of mystery and delight in the presence of God.

## The God-Enriched Man

In Isaiah 45:3, the prophet writes, "And I will give thee the treasures of darkness, and hidden riches of secret places, that thou mayest know that I, the LORD, which call thee by thy name, am the God of Israel." If Shakespeare had written that, he would have said, "The treasures of light." Who would have thought of the treasures of darkness? It took God to think of that. God's ways of enriching a man are certainly not man's ways. God says, "I will enrich you by the darkness and by the very troubles that come to you."

God's idea of blessing is certainly not our idea. God's ways of bringing blessings upon our head are certainly not the ways we would choose. God often hides His blessing in trouble or trial, which makes it all the sweeter when it comes our way.

The three Hebrew children—Shadrach, Meshach and Abednego—never figured that they would find, in Nebuchadnezzar's furnace, God's blessing. Daniel found God's blessing in the den of lions. Every man or woman of faith you can read about in the Scriptures found God's blessing in the trials and troubles of life.

These men and women of faith were not perfect by any stretch of the imagination. Their focus was not on being perfect, but rather on being obedient. Through the vehicle of obedience, the man or woman of faith will be led to that mysterious and wonderful place called the blessing of God.

## A Mighty Fortress Is Our God
Martin Luther (1483–1546)

A mighty Fortress is our God, a bulwark never failing;
Our helper He, amid the flood of mortal ills prevailing:
For still our ancient foe doth seek to work us woe;
His craft and power are great, and, armed with cruel hate,
On earth is not his equal.

Did we in our own strength confide, our striving
    would be losing;
Were not the right Man on our side, the Man of
    God's own choosing:
Dost ask who that may be? Christ Jesus, it is He;
Lord Sabaoth, His Name, from age to age the same,
And He must win the battle.

That word above all earthly powers, no thanks to them,
    abideth;
The Spirit and the gifts are ours through Him Who with
    us sideth:
Let goods and kindred go, this mortal life also;
The body they may kill: God's truth abideth still,
His kingdom is forever.

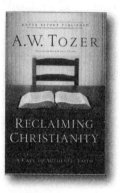
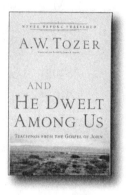
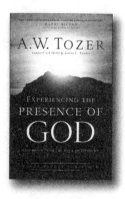

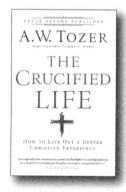